ParaPro Assessment Prep 2022-2023

Study Guide + 270 Questions and Answer Explanations for the ETS Praxis Test (Includes 3 Full-Length Practice Exams)

Table of Contents

Chapter 1: ParaPro Assessment Introduction

This ParaPro Study Guide consists of two sections: theory and practice. The theory section teaches all the key concepts that might appear on the test. The practice section intends to simulate a real-life examination setting to test your skills and learning abilities.

We made this guide easy and reliable. With it, you will be able to excel on your ParaPro exam after a minimum number of hours spent practicing.

The ParaPro Examination

The Educational Testing Service (ETS) offers the ParaPro Evaluation to prospective and practicing academic professionals. It tests your math abilities, reading abilities and writing abilities and assesses whether you can apply this expertise in a classroom environment or not. The test is administered digitally by participating schools.

The Exam Format

The maximum time given to complete the exam is 2.5 hours. It consists of 90 multiple-choice questions that test your reading, writing and math skills. About 70 percent of the examination tests basic skills, while the rest tests your ability to apply your knowledge in a classroom.

Who the ParaPro Examination Is For

The ParaPro Assessment uses a structured examination framework to evaluate how well you can explain primary academic concepts to young minds in the simplest way possible.

When and Where the Test Is Offered

The test is distributed to participating school districts, local education departments and other organizations on a computer or remotely to your personal computer or another safe location. This exam is administered either remotely or at high schools, colleges and education support facilities throughout the year. For available test dates, contact your chosen testing facility directly.

To schedule a remote ParaPro exam, set up an account and register at ProProctor.

The official score report is reported to the education department that received the evaluation, usually two or three weeks after the scheduled assessment.

Test Retake Policy

The ParaPro Assessment may be retaken 28 days after the initial date of the first exam. Tests taken before this time period has passed will not be considered valid.

Test Fee

The test fee is $55.

Certain test centers may charge an extra premium or online testing fee. The remote inspection fee is $91, and the rescheduling fee is $45.50.

Payments are nonrefundable.

If you want to make changes to the date your test is scheduled or any other modifications, you can do so by visiting the test center you are registered at or from your ProProctor account if you intend to take the test from home.

Why You Should Choose This Guide

This guide is dedicated to the teachers who make up an integral part of our high school education system.

We know that learning every single concept in academia can be very hard, and retaining all that information until the exam day is nearly impossible. However, with this guide, you will not have to worry about having all your bases covered.

This is a comprehensive, meticulously researched study guide. We wanted this guide to be easy, reliable and quick so that you could excel with a minimum number of hours spent studying for your ParaPro exam.

This guide addresses the specific areas you need to review in order to ace the ParaPro exam and is guaranteed to help you put your best foot forward on exam day.

All you need is some motivation and the will to prove yourself to the world.

Best of luck to you! Let's begin.

Chapter 2: Reading Skills and Knowledge

Good readers can understand all forms of texts, including tables, graphs and charts. The ParaPro assessment includes reading material designed to assess your understanding of a variety of real-life situations. The following are the areas you need to review in order to pass the reading test.

Text Structure

There are three components of a well-structured text:

1. Introduction

2. Body

3. Conclusion

The type of text decides its structure.

Introduction

An organized text starts with a few introductory sentences. The first sentence of a paragraph is its topic sentence. When writers create an outline for a document, they write the topic sentences first. These single sentences make it easier to fill in the essay later.

The body of a paragraph elaborates upon the topic sentence. It sticks to the paragraph's main idea and does not deviate unless something related to the topic needs to be discussed. This keeps the text focused and well structured.

The topic sentence reflects the main argument of the document. This sentence should serve as a preview of the entire paragraph and provide a clear-cut direction to the paragraph.

Readers can identify the intent of the paragraph by reading the topic sentence.

The main idea

To master reading skills, you need to learn how to find the main idea of a paragraph or document. You need to understand the context of the piece to make an inference and find the document's purpose.

Defining the main idea

The main idea of a passage is the concept that the author wants to communicate to readers. It is the primary point of the passage. Most of the time, the topic sentence states the main idea of the passage. It informs readers what the passage is about. The supporting details make up the rest of the paragraph and add more meaning to the piece of text. The main idea is elaborated across the passage in the form of smaller points.

The main idea serves as an all-encompassing summary for the document. It is usually directly addressed in the topic sentence and does not include specifics of the content. Those details are discussed in the passage's supporting details.

Implied main idea

When the main idea is not directly stated in the topic sentence, it is called the implied main idea. As the main idea is implied instead of being directly stated, the readers need to look at context to determine the author's purpose. They need to use specific words, sentences and images to deduce the author's intent.

Finding the main idea

You need to find the main idea of the document if you want to understand a passage. You can pinpoint the main idea of the passage by doing the following.

Identify the Topic

To find the main idea of the passage, you need to identify the topic first and figure out who or what the text is about.

Find the Crux of the Paragraph

You can figure out the main idea of the passage by summarizing the entire topic in your own words. For that, you need to thoroughly read the paragraph and describe your understanding in one sentence. In 10 to 12 words, express what you have gleaned from the text.

Carefully Read the First and Last Sentences

You can understand a document's intent by looking at its first and last sentences. The main idea is often stated in or near the first or the last line of the paragraph. Carefully read both of these sentences to determine the theme of the passage.

In some cases, the author puts the main idea in the second sentence of the passage. This sentence often starts with words like *but, however* and *on the contrary*. In such passages, the first sentence lays the groundwork for introducing the main idea.

Look for Repeated Ideas

Paragraphs with a lot of information are hard to summarize. To find the main idea of such a document, you should look for repeated ideas, words or phrases.

Find out what the paragraph consistently focuses on. Understand what the author is trying to imply with the repetition of words. It will make it easier to find the main idea.

Supporting Ideas

Once the main idea has been introduced in the topic sentence or the second sentence, the author adds facts, reasons, quotes, examples and statistics to support it. The purpose of body paragraphs is to build upon the topic.

The paragraph starts with the main claim. It states the most important idea that is going to be discussed in the passage. Supporting details serve as evidence that proves the author's claims. Supporting details need to be solid and convincing.

Analysis or evaluation is often used to support the main idea. It connects the evidence provided with the claim. In a paragraph, a connection between ideas is created using transitions. Clear transitions add to the text's flow by helping readers move from one idea to the next.

Author's Purpose

The author's purpose is the "why" behind the writing. It is the reason that inspired the writer to discuss a topic in the first place. Readers need to identify the author's reason and intent. This is how they can make sense of what the author is trying to communicate in the passage.

Types of author's purpose

There are several types of author's purpose. Five of the most important include:

1. Persuasion
2. Information
3. Entertainment
4. Explanation
5. Description.

Let's discuss each of these author's purposes in detail.

Persuasion

Persuasion is commonly used in nonfiction writing. The goal is to persuade readers that what the passage states is true and/or that they should take a specific action.

To identify the author's intent of persuasion, readers need to understand if the writer is trying to convince them of a belief or is asking them to take a particular action. The Readers need to recognize the strategies and tactics that make a document persuasive.

Various signs indicate that a particular piece of writing is persuasive. Some of these signs include repetition, use of supporting evidence, emotive imagery, attacking opposing viewpoints, hyperbole, the use of forceful phrases and more.

Information

When the author's goal is to update the audience about a real-life topic, the author's purpose is to inform. One of the best ways to identify whether or not the author wants to inform is to see if he or she has used facts as supporting ideas.

Note that authors also use facts and statistics when they intend to persuade (rather than inform). However, there is a difference between both of these approaches. When the author's goal is to inform, he or she will state facts to teach the reader. On the contrary, when an author intends to persuade, he or she will share only the facts that support a particular argument.

To identify the author's purpose, readers need to master the ability to recognize hidden intent. This skill can be achieved only through practice. In literary pieces, persuasion is often masked as information.

Entertainment

The author will try to keep things as interesting as possible if the goal is to entertain readers. This type of author's purpose is reflected in fictional writing. The author keeps the readers engaged with sharp dialogue, an action-packed storyline or creative characterization.

Identifying this form of author's purpose is easy. Most of the time, documents intended to entertain are fictional. They do not include real-life facts or statistics.

Fiction writers use a variety of techniques to keep readers engaged. For example, they use cliffhangers to compel readers to read the next chapters. They incorporate drama, humor or mystery into their stories.

Explanation

When the goal of a written passage is to communicate a method or process to readers, the author's purpose is to explain.

An explanatory document is often organized in the form of numbered points or bullets. In such pieces of writing, various imperatives are used. Explanatory pieces also may contain diagrams and illustrations that reinforce what the text states.

Description

Words have the power to take readers beyond one dimension of the picture. Some words describe a scene better than an entire paragraph would.

This form of author's purpose is often observed in fiction writing. Authors use a variety of sensory details to engage a reader's senses. Whether it is a fiction or nonfiction piece, descriptive writing relies significantly on adjectives that engage the reader's imagination.

Theme of a Piece of Writing

The underlying main idea of a literary work is its theme. It can be stated either directly or indirectly. There are two types of themes that appear in literary works: major and minor themes.

An idea that the author repeats throughout the document is the major theme. It is the most significant idea that consistently appears in the document. On the contrary, a minor theme is an idea that only briefly appears in the content. The minor theme of the text is often closely related to the major theme.

Theme vs. subject

Readers often confuse the theme of a document with its subject. The subject of a written piece is the topic that serves as its foundation. The theme is an idea, opinion or viewpoint expressed throughout the document.

For example, the writer might choose war as a topic to discuss. The theme could be the adversities war causes for humanity. Readers can explore the theme by following the plot and analyzing the characters.

How is the theme presented?

Writers have several means through which to present a theme. They can choose to express it through the feelings of the main character toward the subject. Thoughts and conversations between different characters can also be used to present the theme. Events in the story and the characters' actions are also consequential in deciding the text's theme.

What is the author's point of view?

The author must decide the point of view in which to express ideas. There are three options: first person, second person and third person. The reader can identify the author's point of view by looking at the types of pronouns used.

First person

When a character retells or revisits experiences in a text, the narrative is first person. From the first-person point of view, readers know only what the main character knows. *I, me, my, mine, we, our, ours* are used as pronouns in this case.

Second person

The perspective of *you* is used when the story is told in second person. This form of narrative is often followed while giving direction in recipes and instruction manuals.

Third person

When a text is written from the third-person point of view, authors act as detached observers. They tell the story's actions and dialogues from afar. This narrative tells the reader only what is heard and seen. The reader does not learn what the characters feel or believe. The pronouns used in this form of writing include *he, she, it* and *they*.

In literary works, the third-person point of view can be divided into two types:

- **Third-person limited omniscient**

In third-person limited omniscient, the story is told from the perspective of one character only. The reader gets to know only what a particular character thinks, believes, feels, knows, hears and sees. In this form of writing, *he, she, it* and *they* are used as pronouns.

- **Third-person omniscient**

When authors tell a story from the third-person omniscient perspective, they share unlimited information and can describe all characters' thoughts and personalities. They are not limited to a single character when it comes to interpreting behavior. The pronouns in this form of narrative include *he, she, it* and *they.*

How a Text Is Organized

Depending upon the author's purpose, text structure can take a variety of forms. It also depends upon the audience for whom a piece is written. The commonly used text structures include:

Sequence

Most of the time, the author decides to arrange the text sequentially. In this case, the text is organized in the form of steps to explain a process to the readers. Every component of the text represents a step of the overall process.

In this form of text organization, a sequential pattern is followed that takes the reader from the start to the end of a process.

Problem-solution

In this form of text organization, the author addresses a problem and suggests its solution. This text structure consists of two main sections. The first section describes the topic and discusses why it is a problem. It also explains why this problem must be addressed. The second section offers a possible solution to the problem.

Documents with this text structure often end with a challenge that persuades readers to take action. Therefore, it is most commonly used in persuasive writing.

Compare-contrast

This form of text organization is used when the author needs to share the similarities or differences between two or more subjects. Such texts aim to draw a connection for the readers by arranging the information based on the similarities and differences between subjects.

The authors use comparison-contrast to familiarize readers with a lesser-known subject by connecting it to something they already know.

Descriptive

When the author decides to follow spatial or chronological order, it is known as descriptive organization. In this form of text organization, the writer describes events based on location or time. This text structure describes a scene in detail. It addresses one topic at a time. This form of organization is used to present the progression of time to help readers see the bigger picture.

Cause and effect

This format of writing has two parts, the cause and the effect. In the first part, the author introduces an event to the readers as the cause. The second section explains the consequences that take place as a result of the cause.

This format of writing is similar to a problem-solution organization in structure. However, it does not necessarily need to offer a solution. It concerns only the outcomes that take place as the consequence of an event.

Persuasive writing also uses this text structure.

Chapter 3: Application of Reading Skills and Knowledge of Classroom Instruction

Basic Reading Components

Fluent reading requires a combination of various skills. You need to master these skills to become a good reader. A deficit in any of these skills can affect reading ability. Let's discuss the areas a good reader is competent in.

1. Phonemic awareness

Most people confuse phonemics with phonics. These are not the same thing. Phonics concerns associating a sound with a letter, usually the one the word begins with. Phonemic awareness can be developed in various ways. This includes listening to and singing nursery rhymes, identifying the difference between two similar sounds, trying to make different sounds or breaking a word into different sounds.

2. Phonics

You need to develop a good understanding of phonemics before tackling phonics. Once you are aware of phonemics, you can learn how written words are formed.

Phonics studies the common sounds that the letters of the alphabet make. It also includes the sounds produced when these letters are combined. The English language is full of exceptions. Therefore, the letter-sound correspondence does not always apply when words are read. However, phonics serves as a strong foundation that makes word analysis easier.

The knowledge of phonics allows you to sound out unknown words.

3. Fluency

Achieving fluency is vital if you want to read fast and comprehend well. Fluent readers understand a topic well. If you read too slowly, by the time you reach the end of the text, you will forget what you read in the beginning. Therefore, fluent reading is important for overall comprehension.

Fluency can be developed in a variety of ways. You can participate in activities such as plays and choral reading that require you to read aloud. You can also try tape-assisted or partner reading to develop good fluency. Reading the same sentence over and over again also makes you more fluent.

4. Vocabulary

Rich vocabulary means you can read, recognize and understand several words. Readers with a strong oral vocabulary often find it easier to develop an extensive reading vocabulary.

You can expand your vocabulary by reading more literature and getting familiar with new words. Reading literary works with rich oral language can improve your vocabulary.

Vocabulary development also includes the acquisition of basic sight words—words that you identify instantly, such as *the* and *for*. Memorizing sight words improves your fluency, as they regularly appear in text. You can search for lists of sight words online to expand your sight word vocabulary.

5. Comprehension

Being able to just sound words out does not make you a good reader. If you don't understand what you read, the activity is moot. You can gain a deeper understanding of texts through frequent questioning. Recall questions make comprehension easy. You need to learn beyond the deeper meaning of words. You should be able to acquire information from the material you have read. You must learn how to produce an answer from the information provided.

Word Analysis Skills

When readers fail to decipher a word, reading problems occur. This makes it difficult to make sense of a sentence, and comprehension of the entire writing piece is affected. Word analysis skills include:

1. Sounding out words

Sounding out words helps when you find a word difficult to pronounce. When you come across unknown words, you sound them out with the help of letters. For example, if the word is a *car*, you know how Cs, As and Rs sound. You can therefore effortlessly put together a word.

Smoothly making the sound each of the letters makes helps you identify an unfamiliar word's pronunciation.

Consonant sounds

All letters except for *a, e, i, o* and *u* are consonants. Some of these letters make more than one sound. For example, *c* in *cat* is pronounced differently compared to *c* in *city*.

Sometimes, these consonants make an entirely new sound when they are combined with another word. For example, the sound produced when *c* and *h* are combined is *ch,* as in *chart.* However, it does not change when *c* and *h* meet in *chorus.* It can be very confusing at times. However, with practice, it gets easier to pronounce the words where consonants meet.

2. Long and short vowel sounds

There are five vowels: *a, e, i, o* and *u.* Each of these vowels has two different sounds. Various other sounds are also created when they are used in different words and combined with other letters. Sometimes, vowels make an entirely different sound, regardless of the letter behind them. For example, *a* is pronounced differently in *cat, cake, caught* and *what.*

Recognizable rhyming parts

If an unknown word rhymes with a known word, it gets easier to decipher it. For example, *wake* and *cake* sound similar. Recognizable rhyming parts make pronouncing a new word easy. You can substitute the first letter of the known word with that of the new word to decode its pronunciation.

Word parts

Sometimes, bigger words are harder to read as a whole. Therefore, they need to be broken down into smaller parts to understand how they need to be pronounced. There are various techniques for doing so, including:

- **Syllables**

Use your finger to hide all except the first syllable of the word and try to sound out just that part. Move your finger further along the word and keep adding one syllable at a time. Combine all syllables to pronounce the word correctly.

- **Base words**

Base words are also known as root words. Sometimes, a short word is turned into a longer word with additional letters. You can look for a shorter word in the longer one to make it easier to sound out.

- **Prefixes**

Once the root word has been determined, you need to look at the part that comes before that. The word before the root word is the prefix. Examples include *in-, un-* and *pre-.* When applied before the root word, the prefix changes the word's meaning.

- **Suffixes**

Similar to prefixes, suffixes also entirely change the meaning of a word. For example, *-ly*, when added to *neat*, creates the adverb *neatly*.

Compound words

Compounds words are two complete words that are joined to make one longer word. Upon examining a compound word, you will find two short words that make sense even when written individually. Examples include *doghouse*, *somebody* and *lunchbox*.

Context clues

The words around an unknown word serve as a clue. They help you figure out the context of the less familiar word. By looking closely at the rest of the sentence, you can quickly figure out the context in which an unknown word is used.

Word relationships

Sometimes, pointing out the relationship between words makes it easier to read them.

Synonyms

Synonyms are words with the same meaning. However, their connotations are slightly different. They are interchangeable and help writers avoid being repetitive.

Synonyms are also helpful in building vocabulary. They allow you to make a connection between a lesser-known word and a word you are already familiar with.

Antonyms

Antonyms are words that mean the opposite of each other. They are used to present contrast. They also help with vocabulary development. They make it easier to learn new words because it is easy to remember them as the opposite of a word you already know. For example, you can write "the room was very cold" as "the room was not warm."

Antonyms make it easier to express the same idea using an entirely different set of words. That is how they **help you expand your vocabulary.**

Homonyms

Words with the same spellings and pronunciation but different meanings are known as homonyms. The word *yard* is an example of a homonym. According to one definition, a yard means the space around a house ("a party in our yard"). It is also defined as a measurement unit ("I need two yards of fabric to sew my prom dress"). The context decides what *yard* means in a sentence.

Alphabetizing words

Sometimes, putting words in alphabetical order makes it easier to understand them. It helps you recognize the similarities and differences between the words. Choosing words that start with different letters helps expand your vocabulary. You can separate the words that begin with the same letter and then move on to the next.

You can use an alphabetical chart as a reference.

Parts of the Reading Process

Various strategies can help you improve your reading skills. Some of them include:

Prereading strategies

You can enhance the reading experience with prereading strategies. Before reading a book, develop the habit of looking at the cover and the book's back. Flip through the pages to get an idea of what it is about.

You can also look at the pictures on the cover and inside the book to better understand the content. Read the blurb written on the back of the book or the introduction. Each of these steps prepares you for the text you will be reading.

Comprehension questions

You can also ask yourself higher-level questions to evaluate your understanding of a text. Try to understand the purpose behind a piece of writing.

Try to read in a way that encourages deeper thinking. Check your interpretation of the text by backing your understanding with reasoning.

Reading written directions

Before you begin to read a document, it is always better to read the directions to make the reading process easier. The best approach is to read the instructions out loud. Ask yourself what they mean and interpret your understanding in your own words.

Using Resources

Sometimes, to understand a text, you may require additional resources. For example, you might need dictionaries or atlases.

You can use dictionary pages to improve your vocabulary and make the most valuable use of your time. Dictionary skills can significantly improve your reading and learning experience.

Words Used in Context

Sometimes, readers come across words they are unfamiliar with. Such words can be deciphered with the use of context clues. Using context clues includes looking at the words around unfamiliar words. If there is a sentence you find unfamiliar, read the sentences around it to make more sense.

The words surrounding the unfamiliar word will serve as clues that make it easier to find the probable meaning of the unknown word, sentence or phrase.

Difference between Statements and Inferences

The majority of the time, authors make direct statements to the reader. They clearly state what they mean and what they want the readers to take away. However, other times, authors use hints that they want the reader to pick up through the text. They do not directly state what they mean. They want the reader to draw an inference.

An inference is the conclusion that the reader draws based on the clues and hints that the author provides. The reader finds the hidden meaning using deductive reasoning. The inference is not stated outright but is suggested. It is up to the reader how to interpret a message.

Difference between Facts and Opinions

In literary works, opinions are often passed off as facts. To tell facts apart from opinions, critical reading is required. A fact is a statement that has been proven to be true or is accepted as truth. On the other hand, an opinion may or may not be based on facts. It can be an expression of personal thoughts and feelings.

Opinions are often personal. They are not necessarily accepted by society. It is important to identify what is a fact and what is an opinion in a text. It can be misleading if the reader accepts an opinion as a fact. This makes it extremely important for the reader to discern the difference between facts and opinions.

Fallacies in Texts

An unsound argument in a text is referred to as a fallacy. On the surface, such an argument appears well thought out. However, the argument loses its authenticity as soon as it is questioned or tested.

Authors use fallacies when they are trying to persuade their audience. Some of the most commonly used fallacies include:

False analogy

When the author compares two things in the text, it is referred to as an analogy. False analogies are often to persuade. Using false analogies, the writer wants readers to assume that two things are similar in one aspect when they are likely to be the same in all other aspects. When the argument falls apart upon closer investigation, it is referred to as a false analogy.

Circular reasoning

Circular reasoning is used when the author needs to prove that "proof" is the same as a "conclusion." Such arguments are not supported by logical reasoning. They simply go around and around in a circle until an intended conclusion is accepted.

Circular reasoning appears to be sound from the outside. However, upon closer look, there is no substantial proof that supports the argument. It falls apart as soon as it is tested, questioned or challenged.

False dichotomy

This type of fallacy is also referred to as either/or reasoning or false dilemma. In this type of argument, the audience is presented with only two choices (even though multiple options exist). The argument is created for the readers to choose either this or that.

This type of fallacy fails to acknowledge various other options that exist. It discusses only the two extremes instead of multiple dimensions that exist between the two.

Overgeneralization

This type of fallacy occurs when conclusions are based on a single experience or limited sampling. Overgeneralization does not consider the bigger picture. It relies on small evidence. For example, "Tom has been smoking a pack of cigarettes every day for 20 years but is well and alive at 72 years of age." This argument posits that smoking does not kill because Tom did not develop lung or heart disease even after 20 years of smoking. But what about all the other people smoking *has* killed? In overgeneralization, the author uses one exception and turns it into a rule.

Slippery slope

This fallacy is created when the author tries to connect a series of events that are not closely related. The first event is gradually snowballed into a huge issue. The author jumps from one event to another in an attempt to create relevance.

Ad hominem

In this type of fallacy, the author attacks the person making an argument rather than the argument itself. If the author does not have a good counterargument, he or she attacks the person behind it. The author uses an ad hominem fallacy to make it sound like the other person's argument is invalid.

Chapter 4: The Tools of the Reading Process

Prereading involves examining the text before you start reading. This practice makes it easier to make sense of the text you are about to read.

Prereading

Prereading activities include a variety of practices that engage you in the process of discovering the text. The majority of prereading activities are learner-centered. The instructor's job is to look for potential problems that affect the text's readability. After identifying the readability issue, the instructor suggests prereading activities that help students overcome these difficulties.

It is important to identify the source of difficulty to make the reading process easier. Prereading activities help you summarize the content and make more sense out of it.

These activities help you understand the purpose of the text. They help you find the main idea. Prereading provides a picture of what you should expect from the text. It creates a map of what the author wants a reader to take away from the passage.

Prereading improves your actual in-depth reading experience with clues to the content of the text. The reading process becomes more effective if you follow the hints. These clues arouse curiosity and make the reading experience more interesting. The following are some of the prereading activities that make the actual in-depth reading easier.

1.   Consider the title

Start with the title. This is the first step of the prereading process. The title's primary purpose is to tell you what the text is going to be about.

For example, if you are reading a book with the title *The Intelligent Investor*, you can tell a lot about the content by its title:

- It could be written by an investor with years of experience in making successful investments.
- It could be a biography of a successful investor and his struggles.
- It could serve as a guide for new investors to become successful in the market.

The title of the book tells a lot about the content. It prepares you for the text you are about to read. It tells you what to expect from the text. The title of the literary work needs to be closely related to the content inside.

2.   Read the author's name

One of the most important prereading activities is reading the author's name. See if you know the author already and/or if there is anything you know about the person. Most books include a short bio of the author at the beginning or end of the text.

If you do not know the author, google the name before you start reading. If it is a life-skill book, you need to ensure that the author is an acknowledged expert on the topic. The person should have a degree, training or credentials in the subject.

3.   Skim through the text

Skimming the text is another good way to get familiar with the content before reading. Simply going through the headings tells a lot about the text. Pullouts that include highlighted content also serve as a great clue. Headings show the sections a subject has been divided into.

4.   Look for visual clues

Photographs, illustrations, graphs, charts, maps and diagrams serve as visual clues. The captions of images also provide valuable information about the subject.

5.   Look for embedded web links in e-texts

If you are preparing to read an e-text document, look for embedded web links in the file. These links lead to valuable resources that help you better understand the text.

6.   Read the summary of academic texts

The majority of academic texts and essays are similar in structure. Every paragraph starts with a topic sentence that serves as the crux of the entire paragraph. The first sentence summarizes the paragraph. You can understand the written text by going through each paragraph's topic sentence.

Prereading Strategies that Work Best

Various strategies enable you to make the most out of prereading activities. Some of these strategies include:

Outlining expectations

Skim a text and list the questions that come to mind. Your expectation should be to be able to answer these questions once you are done reading. You can outline the answers you find on your way to the end of the text. You can also create blanks that can be filled in as you read the material.

Rating your knowledge

Before reading, students should receive an assignment to rate their understanding of the terms and concepts they will find in the text. Instructors can provide readers with a list of key words or concepts. They can rate students' understanding by using a rubric or rating system. For example, readers can be asked to use a 1–5 scale to denote how much they know on a book about dinosaurs. Readers who rate their knowledge "5" may have a good understanding of the text, while readers who rate their knowledge as "0" may require further prereading activities to enhance their comprehension of the assigned text.

KWHL Chart

A KWHL chart stands for:

- What a student **Knows**
- What a student **Wants** to know
- **How** a student will find the information, and
- What a student has **Learned**.

A chart with an added "How I will find out…" column can help students with the prereading process. Using this strategy, students can write down what they have gleaned from their reading topic.

They can write everything they already know under the K column. They can add everything they want to learn under the W column. They can write how they are supposed to learn what they want to learn under the H column. The L column should be left to be filled in later. Once readers have read the content, they can come back to the L column to write what they have learned.

The teacher can use this strategy to begin a lesson effectively. It can also be used as a prereading activity.

Using a pre-created KWL Chart

Using a pre-created KWL Chart is another great pre-reading strategy. Teachers can provide the students with a KWL Chart or ask students to create one. They can ask them to be as creative as they can. KWL Charts can be created by folding a piece of paper in the form of a letter.

Ask the students to write what they know about the content in the K column. They need to write what they know about the content under the W column. The L column can be used to add what they have learned after reading the text

Creating a List of Possible Sentences

The teacher should create a list of phrases and key terms that frequently appear in the assigned text. This list should be provided to the students. The students should be asked to write a possible sentence using the words and phrases. These sentences should indicate what the students expect to come across in the text.

Use the SQ3R strategy

SQ3R stands for Survey, Question, Read, Recite and Review.

Survey

In this step, students should be asked to survey the document beyond the text. This includes pictures, titles, captions, graphs, charts and more. Students should survey the visual clues first before reading the content.

Question

Students write a question based on what they have learned after their initial survey.

Some of these questions include:

- Who is the author?
- Who is the speaker?
- Who is the author speaking to?
- What is the attitude of the speaker toward the subject being discussed?
- What does the author think about the speaker?
- Do the speaker or the other characters go through major growth or change?
- How does the literary work begin?
- How does the literary work end?
- Were there major elements that recurred?
- Which type of setting is being portrayed?
- Does this piece of work resemble other things you have read?
- What are the similarities and differences you have found?
- Is your paraphrasing an adequate restatement of the original text?
- In what way is the piece written, and how well does it address the topic?
- How have metaphors been used?
- Does the work contain meter, rhyme and alliteration?

Read

Students should be able to read and answer the questions they have written down as they work their way through the assigned text.

Recite

Once the answers have been read, students should be able to recite them without having to go back to look them up.

Review

Students should be able to recall and summarize what they have written once they are done reading.

Word Splash

The teacher should gather key words for a reading assignment. These words can be arranged on a piece of paper to create a "word splash" that students can refer to.

Asking questions about a literary work

While reading a literary work, the reader should read it out loud rather than reading silently. Reading an academic work includes much more than reading just the text. The reader should also look at those elements that make the reading exercise easy. Some of the best techniques include reading footnotes and looking for references and words they should know before in-depth reading.

Once the text has been read, readers should be able to paraphrase the entire piece. This way, they can evaluate their understanding of the subject. Various questions make it possible for the reader to find the crux of a document. The students should try finding the answer to these questions while reading a piece of literature. Before in-depth reading, most of these answers will be wrong. However, they will serve as an outline that tells readers what they need to learn from a document.

Using the Dictionary

The dictionary is one of the most important resources for learning a language. Students can better understand what they read and expand their vocabulary with the effective use of a dictionary. Instructors should teach students how to make effective use of the dictionary to make in-depth reading more interesting and efficient.

Why are dictionary skills important?

Dictionaries are much more than a list of words with their meanings. When used the right way, they improve students' reading abilities. Dictionaries shift some of the responsibility of learning to students.

Dictionary skills are vital in helping readers disentangle information in a document. They help readers better understand text. This reading resource sparks readers' interest and helps them think beyond the meaning of the words.

The use of a dictionary promotes critical thinking. Students can guess the meaning of an unfamiliar word and look it up in the dictionary to see whether they are right or wrong. Dictionaries are helpful when students face difficulties while reading in the absence of teachers.

These reading resources allow students to explore new modes of study. It helps them identify their personal preferences. Students can choose the learning style that best suits them. Dictionaries serve as an ideal tool for solving individual learning problems. They can improve interactive and communicative activities.

How to encourage the use of the dictionary in the classroom

Encouraging the use of the dictionary in the classroom can make learning easier for the students.

The teacher should always look for opportunities where students can develop a better understanding of literary works using a dictionary. Make sure classroom activities are engaging. This way, you can make all students use the dictionary even if they do not want to. Try to conduct enjoyable activities that interest students in using dictionary skills.

Do not limit the use of the dictionary to a separate class session. Try to integrate the dictionary throughout the classwork to make dictionary skills an essential part of students' reading. This way, students will find dictionary work an important part of the language-learning process.

Before designing activities that promote the use of the dictionary, try it yourself first. This way you will learn how long it will take for the student to perform a dictionary work activity. It will also give you an idea of the mistakes students might make while using the dictionary.

Ask your students not to rush while using their dictionaries. Allow time for a false start. Let them make mistakes in selecting words and finding their meanings. You can correct them later. But first, let them learn from their mistakes. Discuss successes and failures with your students.

Set aside five minutes at the end of class to ask students to look through the dictionary. Allow them to explore it however they want. Picture dictionaries are ideal for beginners. They spark readers' interest and keep them engaged.

Before starting a lesson, make a list of words that students will come across in a chapter. Ask students to look up the meanings of these words beforehand. This strategy will help them better understand what is being taught.

If it is not a critical test, allow students to use dictionaries. Since the dictionary makes the natural learning process easier, students should be allowed to use it whenever they need it. Once the test is finished, you can ask students to improve their mistakes using dictionaries. They should turn in the test once they have fixed the mistakes. This will help them realize how a dictionary can help them with learning problems.

You can improve students' dictionary skills by setting vocabulary goals for them. Ask them to find three to five new words of their choice every day. Encourage students to discuss the words they have learned with other students.

Once students are consistently using a dictionary as part of their reading practice, monitor if they are using it correctly and effectively. Also ensure that there is a healthy balance between dependence on and independence from the dictionary.

How to interpret written instructions

Written instructions are the directions that explain a procedure or task that needs to be performed. Effective written instructions are supported with visual elements that include images, flowcharts, pie charts, graphs, maps and diagrams. These visual features make it easier to interpret written instructions.

Before performing a task, it is important to understand written instructions clearly. These instructions serve as a guide for the student to accurately complete an assignment. Various steps make it easier for readers to follow written instructions. Some of them include:

Identifying the Nature of the Task

Students need to understand the nature of the task before performing it. To be successful, students should:

Look at the instructions

Students should read the directions and understand what the author wants. Does the author want them to explain, evaluate, discuss or analyze a task?

Identify the topic

Certain content words help identify the topic of the task. Students should carefully read these words before performing the task.

Figure out key words and phrases

Once students have figured out the main thrust of the task, they need to look for the key words and phrases that enable them to make sense of the text.

Determine the scope

Students should find words in the content that clarify its scope, including *refer to examples, focus on* or *confine your discussion to.*

Chapter 5:Mathematical Knowledge and Skills

Fundamentals of Mathematics

The fundamentals of mathematical knowledge include deriving the sum, difference, product and quotient of positive whole numbers. The basic arithmetic operations studied in mathematics include addition, subtraction, multiplication and division. These operations are also associated with arithmetic properties. These properties include commutative, associative and distributive.

The following are the key terms students need to know before learning the basics of mathematics:

Associative property

This refers to a mathematical result that derives the same result regardless of how the elements are grouped.

Commutative property

This is a binary operation that derives the same result when operands' order is changed. It includes addition and multiplication.

Product

When two quantities are multiplied, the result is called the product.

Quotient

The result yielded when one quantity is divided by the other is known as the quotient.

Sum

When two similar or different quantities are added, the result is known as the sum.

Difference

When one quantity is subtracted from the other, the result is referred to as the difference.

Arithmetic Operations

In mathematics, there are four arithmetic operations. All of them are discussed below:

Addition

The most basic of all arithmetic operations is addition. In this operation, two or more quantities are combined into one. The result is the sum. For example, if you have two apples and you borrow three more from a friend, you will have a total of five apples. This idea can be represented in mathematical terms as:

$2 + 3 = 5$

Subtraction

The opposite of addition is subtraction. In this operation, one quantity is removed from another to find the difference between the two. Let's use the same example we used before. Imagine you have five apples, and your friend asks you to return the three apples you borrowed. How many apples will you be left with?

If you remove three apples from five, you will get only two. This idea can be represented in mathematical terms as:

$5 - 3 = 2$

Multiplication

Multiplication combines two or more quantities into one. The result is the product. In most cases, multiplication is considered a consolidation of additions.

When x and y are multiplied, the result is the sum obtained when x is added together y times. Let's learn this concept with the help of an example. Imagine you have four pairs of apples. This idea can be expressed in mathematical terms as:

$2 + 2 + 2 + 2 = 8$

The quicker way to count the apples is to multiply the quantities. In mathematical terms, it will be written as

$2 \times 4 = 8$

No matter which method you use, the result will be the same. Multiplication is mostly used to count items because it is easier to calculate larger quantities or groups when they are multiplied.

Division

This arithmetic operation is the inverse of multiplication. You do not find a larger value by multiplying specific values; instead, you split a larger quantity into smaller values. The result of the division is the quotient. For example, how many pairs are there in a basket of eight apples? The answer is four.

In mathematical terms, this idea can be expressed as:

$8 \div 4 = 2$

Basic Arithmetic Properties

There are three types of basic arithmetic properties.

Commutative property

The commutative property is an arithmetic property in which the order of numbers involved in the equation does not affect the result. There are two commutative operations in mathematics: addition and multiplication. The following examples will better explain this idea:

$4 + 8 = 12 = 8 + 4$

$4 \times 8 = 32 = 8 \times 4$

The commutative property does not include subtraction and division.

Associative property

The associative property is a form of arithmetic property in which the result is not affected by the way numbers are grouped. Just like a commutative property, this arithmetic property also includes addition and multiplication. Both of these operations are associative. The following example will make this idea clearer:

$(6 + 4) + 5 = 15 = 6 + 4 + 5$

$(3 \times 2) \times 2 = 12 = 3 \times (2 \times 2)$

The associative property also does not include division and subtraction.

Distributive property

The distributive property is an arithmetic property in which the sum of two quantities is multiplied by another quantity. An example is:

$(2 + 6) \times 3 = 2 \times 3 + 6 \times 3 = 18$

Negative Numbers

According to specific rules, arithmetic operations can also be performed on negative numbers. Numbers with values less than zero are known as negative numbers. All four arithmetic operations can be performed on negative numbers. Let's discuss each of them one by one.

Addition of negative numbers

The addition of two or more negative numbers is the same as that of two positive numbers. However, a few rules apply. For example:

-4 + -3 = -7 = -3 + -4

Adding two negative numbers yields a bigger negative number. Negative numbers are also referred to as debt. Therefore, the addition of two debts results in a bigger debt. In equations where both negative and positive numbers appear, the negative numbers are written as positive quantities that need to be subtracted. In mathematical terms, this can be represented as in this example:

8 + (-4) = 4 = 8 − 4

In this equation, a credit of 8 is added to a debt of 4. As a result, a credit of 4 is yielded. However, if the value of a negative number is bigger, the result will have a negative sign.

-8 + 4 = -4

-7 + 2 = -9

In this equation, the debt is of higher value than the credit. Therefore, the sum is a negative value. However, the result will be positive if the credit is of higher value than that of the debt.

Subtraction of negative numbers

A negative result is obtained when positive numbers are subtracted from one another. Let's explain this with an example.

5 − 8 = -3

The subtraction of a positive number is the same as that of the addition of the number's negative. In mathematical terms, it can be expressed as in the following example:

$6 + (-8) = -2 = 6 - 8$

$(-3) - 5 = (-3) + (-5) = -8$

Similarly, when negative numbers are subtracted, the same result is yielded when the positive of the same number is added. This idea can be explained in mathematical terms as:

$3 - (-5) = 3 + 5 = 8$

$(-5) - (-8) = (-5) + 8 = 3$

Multiplication of negative numbers

There is a different set of rules to be followed when it comes to multiplying negative numbers. Some of these rules include:

- The result yielded by the multiplication of two positive numbers is positive.
- If a positive and a negative number are multiplied, the product is negative.
- When two negative numbers are multiplied, the product is positive.

These rules can be better explained with the following examples:

$2 \times 3 = 6$

When -2 is added three times, the result is -6.

$(-2) \times 3 = (-2) + (-2) + (-2) = -6$

However,

$(-2) \times (-3) = 6$

Losing the debt is equal to gaining credit. In the example mentioned above, the loss of two debts of three is equal to gaining six credits.

Division

The rule for dividing negative numbers is the same as the rule for multiplying them. Some of these rules include:

- A positive result is obtained when two positive numbers are divided.
- A negative result is yielded when a positive number is divided by a negative number.
- The division of two negative number results in a positive number.

The result is always positive when the signs of divisor and dividend are the same. In mathematical terms, this concept can be represented as:

$6 \div 2 = 3$

$(-6) \div 2 = -3$

However, $(6) \div (-2) = 3$

Additional Rules to Be Considered

Basic arithmetic properties, including commutative, associative and distributive, apply to negative numbers. This concept can be better explained with the help of an example:

$-3 (2 + 5) = (-3) \times 2 + (-3) \times 5$

This example shows the distributive properties of negative numbers.

Fractions

In mathematics, a part of a whole is referred to as a fraction. A fraction is composed of an integer and a non-zero integer. The two components of a fraction include a numerator and a denominator.

The top number of a fraction is known as an integer nominator, and the bottom number of a fraction is referred to as a non-integer denominator. Examples of fractions include 1/2, 3/4 and 5/6.

The numerator indicates equal parts of the whole number written as the denominator. The denominator represents the number of parts needed to create a whole.

Addition of like fractions

There is an entirely different set of rules when it comes to adding fractions. The most important rule is to add only those fractions that have the same denominator.

A quarter of a fraction is written as 1/4. The nominator, which is 1, represents a single quarter. The denominator, which is 4, represents the number of quarters required to make a whole. Let's look at an example.

Imagine you have two quarters. You borrow another three quarters from your friend. By adding both, you get a total of five quarters. One dollar contains four quarters. In mathematical terms, this equation can be represented as

$2/4 + 3/4 = 5/4 = 1\ 1/4$

Addition of unlike fractions

Unlike fractions are fractions whose denominators are different. The denominators need to be the same in order to add unlike fractions.

The easiest way to achieve common denominators is to multiply the denominators of both of the fractions. The numerator of each of the fractions should be multiplied by the same number its denominator is multiplied by. Doing so will ensure that the fraction represents the same ratio.

This idea can be explained better with the following example.

Both fractions need to be converted to 12 while adding a quarter to thirds.

$1/3 + 1/4 = 1\ x\ 4/3\ x\ 4 + 1\ x\ 3/4\ x\ 3 = 4/12 + 3/12 = 7/12$

In algebraic terms, the following expression can be expressed as:

$a/b + c/d = ad + cb/bd$

This method is best when it comes to converting the denominators to the same value. However, there is another faster method. You can also find the least common denominator or smaller denominator to get the same value for denominators.

Addition of fractions to whole numbers

Fractions can also be added to whole numbers. All you need to do is to write the whole number in the form of a fraction. In this case, you need to consider the denominator of the whole number as 1. After doing so, you can continue with the process of addition of fractions mentioned above.

Subtraction of fractions and whole numbers

The subtraction of fractions is similar to addition. You need to convert the denominators of each of the fractions to the same value. This means you should find a common denominator for each of the fractions. Once you have a common denominator, you can subtract the numerators. This idea can be better explained with the following example:

$2/3 - 1/2 = 2\ x\ 2/3\ x\ 2 - 1\ x\ 3/2\ x\ 3 = 4/6 - 3/6 = 16$

You need to rewrite the whole as a fraction if you want to subtract a fraction from the whole number or vice versa. Once done, you can use the method mentioned above for subtracting fractions.

Multiplication of fractions with whole numbers

Multiplication of fractions does not require the denominators to be the same. Just multiply the numerator of one fraction by the other's numerator and the denominator of one fraction by the denominator of the other. For example:

2/3 x 3/4 = 6/12

Division of fractions by the whole number

Multiply a whole number by the reciprocal of a fraction to divide it by a fraction. When you turn the fraction upside down, the result is its reciprocal. The numerator becomes the denominator, and the denominator becomes the numerator. For example:

1/2 ÷ 3/4 = 1/2·4/3 = 4/6 = 2/ 3

Chapter 6: Mathematical Knowledge and Skills, Mental Math and Algebraic Concepts

Calculating percentages is one of the basics of mathematical knowledge. Even though there are percentage calculators available online, everyone should know how to calculate percentages manually. The ParaPro test requires you to calculate percentages without any digital assistance.

Percentage

The word *percentage* is a combination of two words, *per* and *cent*. The word *cent* is an old European word that finds its origin in French, Italian and Latin. The meaning of *cent* is "a hundred." This means the word *percent* is directly translated as "per hundred." Let's simplify it with an example.

Fifty percent means 50 out of 100. If it rained 20 times in 100 days, this means that it rained 20 percent of the time. There are two different formats for writing the numbers that need to be converted into a percentage:

- Decimals
- Fractions.

Converting Decimals into Percentages

It is relatively easy to calculate percentages. A decimal can be converted into a percentage with simple multiplication. All you need to do is multiply the decimal number by 100. Let's look at an example.

You have scored 67 out of 100 on your math quiz. To find the percentage, you need to convert 0.67 to a percentage. To do so, multiply the decimal number by 100.

0.67 x 100 = 67

This means you have scored 67%.

Converting fractions into percentages

Converting fractions into percentages is also very easy. All you need to do is to divide the numerator with the denominator. For example, if the fraction number is 67/100, divide 67 by 100.

67 ÷ 100 = 0.67

Now that the fraction has been converted into a decimal, follow the method mentioned above. Multiply the decimal by 100 to calculate the percentage.

$0.67 \times 100 = 67$

Your answer will be 67%.

Most of the time, numbers do not fit neatly into 100. In such cases, it's harder to calculate the percentage. You can also calculate the given number if you know the percentage. For example, 20% of your salary goes to tax. If you are wondering how much money 20% of your salary is, you need to convert the percentage into decimal form.

Calculating a number out of a percentage is the reverse of calculating the percentage. To do so, you need to divide the percentage provided by 100. Let's follow the example above. To calculate 20% of your income, divide 20 by 100 or 0.20.

$20 \div 100 = 0.20$

Once you have converted the percentage into a decimal number, the result should be multiplied by the given number. In the above case, multiply the result by your total salary. Let's suppose your salary is $750. Multiply the amount by 0.20.

$750 \times 0.20 = 150$

The result is 150. This means that out of $750, you need to pay $150 as tax.

Let's take another example.

Suppose you need to save 25% of your salary to build an emergency fund. If your salary is $1,000, how much money do you need to save out of that?

First, you need to convert 25% into a decimal number. To do that, divide by 100.

$25 \div 100 = 0.25$

The answer is 0.25. Now all you need to do is to multiply the result with your salary, which is $1,000.

$1,000 \times 0.25 = \$250$

This means you need to save $250 out of your current salary to create an emergency fund.

Powers and Exponents

Calculating expressions like 5 x 5 is something we all know. However, it is not the only way to write this expression. There is a shorter way to write the same expression using exponents. Let's take a look at the example below:

5 x 5 = 5^2

If an expression indicates the repeated multiplication of the same factor, it is known as the power. The number being multiplied several times is the base. The exponent is the number of times the base has been used as a factor.

In the case mentioned above, the base number is 5. Its exponent is 2, and the power is 5. Let's learn this concept with a few examples.

How to write 5 x 5 x 5 exponentially

5 x 5 x 5 = 5^3

How to write 4 x 4 x 4 x 4 x 4 exponentially

4 x 4 x 4 x 4 x 4 = 4^5

How to multiply powers

Two powers can be multiplied if they have the same base number. When two powers are multiplied, their exponents are added. In mathematical terms, this idea can be expressed as:

$x^a \times x^b = x^{a+b}$

Let's look at an example:

$3^5 \times 3^4 = 3^{5+4} = 3^9$

How to divide powers

Powers can be divided only if they have the same base number. Exponents are subtracted when powers are divided. In mathematical terms, this idea can be expressed as:

$x^a \div x^b = x^{a-b}$

Let's learn this idea with an example:

$3^2 \div 3^5 = 3^{2-5} = 3^{-3}$

A negative exponent is like that of the reciprocal of a positive exponent. The result above can be written as:

$3^{-3} = 1/3^3$

Performing Mathematical Operations

Calculations in which two numbers need to be added, subtracted, multiplied and divided are simple to perform. You perform one mathematical operation, and you have your answer. However, not all mathematical problems are easy to solve. Various equations require addition, subtraction, division and multiplication at the same time.

For such equations, you need to follow specific mathematical rules to obtain the correct answers.

Mathematics is based on logic. To figure out which operation to perform first in a complex equation, follow a few simple rules. This helps you find out which calculations need to be done first.

The order in which a mathematical equation with multiple operations needs to be solved is known as the order of operations.

Order of Operations

In mathematics, PEMDAS is followed to figure out the order of operations:

Parentheses

According to the rule of operations, the calculation inside the parentheses needs to be performed first.

Exponents

Once the parentheses have been solved, numbers with powers or square roots are simplified.

Multiplication

Multiplication should be the next operation performed.

Division

Next, divide as necessary.

Addition

After division, addition is performed.

Subtraction

Subtraction is the last arithmetic operation performed in an equation.

Using PEMDAS

Solving parentheses

According to PEMDAS, parentheses need to be solved first. You need to calculate the equation within the parentheses from left to right. Let's simplify this concept with the help of an example:

4 x (4 + 2) = ?

Solve the parentheses first:

4 x (6) = ?

4 x 6 = 24

If you ignore these rules and solve the equation from left to right, you will get the wrong answer.

4 x (4 + 2) = ?

16 + 2 = 18

This shows that the parentheses make the biggest difference while calculating the answer to a complex equation.

Solving exponents

Once parentheses are solved, it is time to solve the exponents. Exponents are anything with a square root or a power. Again, you need to work from left to right if there is more than one figure with powers or a square root. For example,

$2^2 + 5 = ?$

In this equation, you need to simplify the power first before adding 5 to the result.

$2^2 + 5 = ?$

2 x 2 + 5 = ?

4 + 5 = 9

Solving multiplication and division

Here is an example of solving multiplication and division.

4 x 2 + 8 ÷ 2 = ?

Multiply first.

4 x 2 = 8

Next, divide.

8 ÷ 2 = 4

Now that you have a simple equation, you can easily find the answer.

Solving addition and subtraction

The last operations you need to solve in a complex equation are addition and subtraction. Work from left to right. For example,

2 + 4 − 5 + 6 = ?

Solve the equation step by step:

2 + 4 − 5 + 6 = ?

6 − 5 + 6 = ?

1 + 6 = ?

1 + 6 = 7

The answer to this complex equation is 7.

Solving a complex equation using PEMDAS

$2 + 6^2 \times (20 \div 5) = ?$

We solve the parentheses first.

$2 + 6^2 \times (4) = ?$

Now we simplify the exponents:

$2 + 6 \times 6 \times (4) = ?$

$2 + 36 \times 4 = ?$

Then, we perform multiplication.

$2 + 144 = ?$

In the last step of this equation, we perform addition.

$2 + 144 = 146.$

Chapter 7: Mathematical Knowledge and Skills, Geometry and Measurement

The Time Value of Money

The time value of money is money that you own, which is more than its future identical sum. The reason is its potential earning capacity. According to this finance principle, money can earn interest. The money that you earn is worth more if you earn it sooner rather than later. As time passes, the value of your money keeps increasing. The time value of money (TVM) is also known as present discounted value.

According to this concept, rational investors would want to receive money in the present. This is because they can earn more interest on the existing amount. This amount will not have an equal worth if it is received in the future. The value of money increases over time. Let's take an example.

When you deposit money into a savings account, you receive a certain percentage as interest. It compounds in value based on the set interest rate.

Why is the time value of money important?

• The time value of money is the concept of having money in the present rather than in the future because of its potential to grow.
• Money is more valuable in the present. This is because of compounding as you receive interest.
• The time value of money can be derived using the payment today, its value in the future, the interest rate and the time.
• The time value of money depends upon the number of compounding periods within each time frame.

Converting One Unit into Another

Units of measurement can easily be converted from one to another. All you need to do is multiply the old unit by a specific form of 1.

How to convert meters into centimeters

A meter is the basic unit of length. It can be defined as the distance a beam of light covers in a matter of seconds. There are many variations of a meter. These variations can be converted from one form to another with simple calculations. These include kilometers, centimeters and millimeters.

1,000 meters = 1 kilometer

1 meter = 100 centimeters

1 meter = 1,000 millimeters

Kilometers per hour (km/h) can be easily converted to meters per second. All you need to do is know the value of the basic units. One kilometer contains 1,000 meters. Similarly, there are 3,600 seconds in an hour.

A kilometer has 1,000 meters and an hour has 3,600 seconds, so a kilometer per hour is:

$1,000 \div 3,600 = 0.2777$ m/s.

You need to perform the conversion as fractions to convert one unit into another or the other way around.

Let's begin with a simple example: converting kilometers into meters.

We know there are 1,000 meters in 1 kilometer. We need to follow a system to make the conversion of units easier. According to this system, the conversion should be written as a fraction that is equal to 1.

- Multiply it and leave behind the units in the answer.
- The units that appear in both the denominator and numerator should be canceled out.

The conversion of the fraction equals 1 and could be written as:

1,000 m/1 km = 1

The entire fraction will be multiplied by 1, as it will not affect the answer. To convert 6 kilometers into meters, you need to multiply by 1:

6 km × 1 = 6 km

After doing so, perform the following calculation:

6 km × 1,000 m/1 km = 6,000 km.

The conversion is not complete yet. The unit that appears in both the denominator and the numerator will be canceled.

6,000 *km x m*/1 km = 6,000 m

From the above equation, it appears that 6 km is equal to 6,000 m. This was easy to figure out. However, you still need a system to follow when calculations become more complex. A neater answer can be derived when the units from the top and bottom of the fraction are canceled.

Let's look at another example. Here, we will convert km/h to m/s using the method above. There are two steps to perform in this conversion.

In the first step, the kilometers per hour will be converted to meters per hour. In the second step, the meters per hour will be converted to meters per second.

Converting km/h to m/h

1 km/h × 1,000 m/1 km = 1,000 km x m / 1 h x km

The units that appear at both the bottom and the top will be canceled.

1,000 km x m/1 h x km = 1,000 *m*/ 1 h

Using this calculation, you can convert km/h into m/h.

Conversion of m/h into m/s

To convert meters per hour to meters per second, you need to consider 1 hour as 3,600 seconds. Hour (h) needs to be on the top so that it can be canceled.

1,000 m/1 h × 1 *h*/3,600 s = 1,000 m x h/3,600 h x s

Now it is time to cancel out the units on the top and bottom.

1,000 m x *h*/ 3,600 h x s = 1,000 *m*/3,600 s

So, the answer in this case is,

1,000 m/3,600 s = 0.2777 m/s.

With experience and practice, you can perform this calculation using the following method:

1 km/1 h x 1,000 m/1 km × *1* h/*3,600 s*

= 1,000 km x m x h/*3,600* h x km x s

= 1,000 m/3,600 s

You can cross out the units as you go in the following way:

$1\ km/1\ h \times 1{,}000\ m/1\ km \times 1\ h/3{,}600\ s = 1{,}000\ m/3{,}600\ s$

Now we will look at an example with a real-life conversion. Suppose you need to convert 80 mph into meters per second. Use the following method to perform this conversion:

$80\ miles/h \times 1{,}609\ m/mile \times 1\ h/3{,}600\ s$

$= 80 \times 1{,}609\ miles\ x\ m\ x\ h\ /\ 3{,}600\ h\ x\ miles\ x\ s$

$= 35.75\ m/s.$

How to convert inches into feet

It is very simple to convert inches into feet. Just divide inches by 12. The reason is one foot contains 12 inches.

Feet = inches ÷ 12

Let's simplify it with an example. Let's convert 48 inches to feet using the formula mentioned above.

Feet = 48 ÷ 12
Feet = 4

Classifying Simple Geometric Forms

Geometry is one of the oldest branches of mathematics. It deals with the properties of space. These properties concern the distance, size, shape and position of geometric figures. A mathematician who studies geometry is known as a geometer.

Geometric Shapes

There are various principle geometric plane shapes. Some of them include:

The Circle

The shape formed when a curve is traced is known as a circle. The distance of the curve from the center point always remains the same, and the circumference of a circle is the distance around the circle. The following formulas can be used to find the perimeter of a circle:

Perimeter of a circle = $P = C = 2\pi r = \pi d$

In the equation above, r is the radius of the circle, and d is its diameter.

The area of the circle can be derived using the following formula:

Area of circle = πr^2

Here, r is the radius of the circle.

The Triangle

When three straight lines are joined together, a triangular shape is formed. These lines are also known as sides. Triangles can be classified into different types based on their sides and angles. The perimeter of a triangle can be found using the following formula:

Perimeter of triangle = a + b + c

In this equation, a, b and c are three sides of a triangle.

The area of a triangle can be derived using the following formula:

Area of triangle = 1/2 bh

Here, b and h are the base and height of a triangle.

Types of triangles according to angles

There are three types of triangles according to angles:

Right-angled triangle

The largest angle of a right-angled triangle is the right angle.

Acute-angled triangle

The largest angle of this triangle is acute, which means it is less than 90 degrees.

Obtuse-angled triangle

The largest of all angles in this triangle is an obtuse angle. It is over 90 degrees.

Types of triangles based on their sides

Based on their sides, there are three types of triangles:

Equilateral triangle

In this type of triangle, all sides are the same length

Isosceles triangle

In this type of triangle, two or more sides have the same length. This means an equilateral triangle is also an isosceles triangle.

Scalene triangle

In this type of triangle, no two sides have equal lengths.

The Rectangle

A shape that has four sides is known as a rectangle. The major property of a rectangle is that all of its angles are 90 degrees. The perimeter of a rectangle can be found by using the following formula:

$P = 2(L + W)$

In this equation, L is the length, and W is the width of a rectangle's sides.

The area of the rectangle can be found using the following formula

Area of rectangle = LW

L and W are the length and width of a rectangle.

The Rhombus

When four straight lines join together, a rhombus is formed. All of its sides are the same. However, unlike triangles, none of its angles measure 90 degrees.

The Square

A square is similar in shape to that of a rectangle and a rhombus. It exhibits the properties of both of the shapes. Each of the angles of a square is a right angle, and all of the sides of a square are equal in length. The perimeter of the square can be found using the following formula:

The perimeter of a square = 4s

In this equation, s is the side of the square.

The area of a square can be found using the following formula:

Area of a square = s^2

In this equation, s indicates the side of the square.

The Trapezoid

A trapezoid has four sides. Two of its sides are parallel, whereas the other two are not.

The area of a trapezoid can be found using the following formula:

Area of trapezoid = $b_1 + b_2/2$ x h

In this equation, b_1 and b_2 are the trapezoid's parallel sides' lengths, whereas h indicates the distance or the parallel sides' height.

X-Y Axis

An x-y axis is also referred to as a Cartesian coordinate system or a coordinate plane. It is a two-dimensional point plane. These points are uniquely defined using a pair of coordinates. Two numbers define every point on the plane, and each of these coordinates calculates the distance of a particular point from the y-axis to the x-axis.

The x-axis and y-axis

The y-axis is a vertical line and can be measured like a stick. You count how far up or down a point is from the x-axis. The x-axis is a horizontal line. To measure a point on the x-axis, you count the distance from the left or right.

Chapter 8: Mathematical Knowledge and Skills

Graphs

A graph is a diagram that displays data and represents the relationship between certain objects. A general trend can be determined by carefully reading a graph. A graph is normally used to relate the results of an experiment to its hypothesis. It is also essential for paving the way to prove a hypothesis with future experiments.

Before analyzing a graph, you need to understand why the information presented is vital to the experiment and comprehend the question's context through the graph. There are several types of graphs. They can present a single set of data in a variety of ways.

Types of Graphs

Students must possess the ability to distinguish various types of graphs. Some of the most common types of graphs include:

Picture graphs

This type of graph uses pictures to represent values.

Bar graphs

In this graph, horizontal or vertical bars are used to display values.

Line graphs

Here, lines are used to display different values.

Scatterplots

This form of graph displays data with the help of scattered points. Once the values are defined on the plot, a line is drawn to connect all points.

How to Interpret a Graph

We can interpret a graph with the help of its title and the axes of the graph. It helps readers figure out which type of graph they are reading. It also helps them understand the nature of the data presented through the graph.

A graph presents the independent variables on the x-axis. These values can be changed. The y-axis displays dependent variables. These variables depend upon the independent variables. For example, a graph that measures a pea plant's height over six months will have weeks on the x-axis and the pea plant's height on the y-axis.

How to determine the general trend of a graph

To better understand the results represented by a graph, the trend of the graph should be determined. Let's take the example of a picture graph. The line with the highest number of pictures will determine the trend. In a bar graph, the trend can be determined by identifying the highest bar. On a line or scatterplot, you need to find the slope of the line.

The slope will be positive if the line points to the upper right corner. On the contrary, the slope is negative if the line points to the lower right corner.

Identification of points that do not fit the trend

There will be various data points that will not fit the general trend. Identify such points and keep track of them. If it is only one bar or one dot in a line that seems out of place, it will not significantly affect the conclusion derived through the graph's analysis.

Tables

A table features rows and columns in which numbers and words are displayed. Tables allow quick and easy comparison of objects or values. They make interpretation and access to information easy. Tables can also show the rise and fall of trends if they are arranged in chronological order. However, they do not provide the most authentic results.

If you want a more dramatic visualization of data, refer to graphs and charts. They give you a more detailed review of the information displayed.

Using tables

Tables are most commonly used to display numerical data. They allow you to compare an object in terms of various characteristics, including length, height, depth, weight and more. A table is the best data visualization tool to display simple data.

What is a matrix?

A matrix is a special type of table that does not compare numerical values. Rather, it compares qualitative data in rows and columns. This qualitative data can be written in words.

A matrix can compare objects in terms of their qualities, such as cost, speed, warranty and more. These items can be products or services. A matrix is used to display words that represent qualitative data.

How to format a table

A table is one of the simplest data visualization tools that display data in rows and columns. Every column is titled with a heading. The heading identifies the content this particular row displays. Most of the time, its contents include measurement units.

The left edge of the table displays headings of the row. These headings define the content that will be displayed in that row. More complex tables have rows and columns subdivided into smaller categories.

Why Charts and Graphs Are Used

Another way to present detailed data is through charts. Graphs and charts are less precise compared to tables.

Graphs not only represent data but also show the trend it follows. Tables only show an amount of data, and it is hard to find a proper pattern displayed by the information. However, a line in a graph shows the overall trend followed over a specific period. There are various kinds of graphs and charts, including horizontal bar charts, pie charts and vertical bar charts.

How to format charts and graphs

Line graphs and bar charts have two axes. The x-axis displays independent variables, and the y axis displays the variables dependent upon the independent variables. Points are plotted on such graphs.

Bar charts and line graphs often use unique colors, shading and more. Before analyzing these charts, the reader must know what these colors show. For that, they should read the chart key.

Mean, Median and Mode

What is mean?

The average of a set of data is known as its mean.

What is mode?

The number that most frequently appears in a set of data is known as the mode.

What is the median?

The middle of the given set of numbers is its median.

How to differentiate between mean and median

The mean and median both indicate the center of the set of data. It is also stated as the central tendency in statistics. However, both are entirely different numbers. Let's make it clear with the help of an example. Imagine we have a list of numbers that includes:

10, 10, 20, 40, 70

The informal average of this set of numbers is its mean. To find the mean, you need to add all numbers. Once you have the sum, divide it by the number of items present in the list.

10 + 10 + 20 + 40 + 70 / 5 = 30

To find the median, arrange the numbers in ascending order. This means you have to write the lowest number first, working your way to the highest number. Now you need to find the exact middle. The middle number of the list is its median. In this case, this number is 20.

There are a few cases in which the mean and median are the same. We can understand that better with the help of an example. Imagine you have a data set that includes numbers 1, 2, 4, 6, 7.

The mean of this data set will be calculated as follows:

1 + 2 + 4 + 6 + 7 / 5 = 4

The median of this set of numbers is 4.

What is the difference between mean and average?

The average is the middle value in a set of numbers. Let's use an example to explain this idea better. Suppose the set of numbers you have is:

10, 6, 20

The average of this set can be found as follows:

10 + 6 + 20 = 36 ÷ 3 = 12

In statistics, this concept is a little different when compared to mathematics. In this field, the average is known as the mean. The reason for the difference in words is that both words are synonyms. The word *mean* is short for arithmetic mean in statistics. The mean is used instead of *average* in statistics because there are several *means* in this field of study. Each of them has a different purpose.

The Most Commonly Used Means in Statistics

There are various types of means students of statistics come across. Each of these means has a very narrow meaning:

Mean of the sampling distribution

This mean is for probability distribution. It is often used with the central limit theorem, which is a set of distributions.

Sample mean

The average value in a sample is known as its sample mean.

Population mean

The average value in a population is referred to as the population mean.

Calculating Mode

The number that most frequently appears in a set of numbers is its mode. Let's look at an example. Suppose the set of the numbers we have is:

21, 21, 21, 23, 24, 26, 26, 28, 29, 30, 31, 33

Now we need to figure out the number that most frequently appears in this set. After analyzing this set, we observe that this number is 21. So, 21 is the mode.

Calculating Median

The middle number of a set of numbers is its median. Before finding the median of the given set of data, the data should be arranged in ascending order. Here is an example:

Imagine the set of numbers you have is:

23, 24, 26, 26, *28*, 29, 30, 31, 33

It has already been arranged in ascending order. Now, find the middle number of this set. The median of this set of numbers is 28. If the set of numbers is even, the average of two of the middle numbers will be the median of the set. For example, imagine the set of numbers you have is:

23, 24, 26, 26, *28, 29*, 30, 31, 33, 34

The median can be calculated as follows:

28 + 29 ÷ 2 = 28.5.

Why Mean, Median and Mode Are Important in Day-to-Day Life

We live in a technology-driven world where information is our biggest asset. Keeping track of data is important in every aspect of life. Whether you want to count the number of students in a class or calculate a company's average revenue, you will need to know how to calculate median and mode.

In our day-to-day life, every number counts. However, it may be hard to process a lot of information without a proper system in place. Mean, median and mode make data-processing easy. Each of these concepts serves as a valuable tool for analyzing a group of data.

Chapter 9: Mathematical Knowledge and Skills

Implementing Basic Knowledge of Mathematics

Formal mathematics requires students to understand basic mathematical concepts. They should be familiar with classification, conservation, ordering and one-to-one correspondence. They should know quality attributes such as shape, weight and sizes before tackling general quantities. They also need to familiarize themselves with numbers and number systems. After learning the basic concepts, solving more complex problems should become easier.

Classification

Classification is one of the earliest concepts of mathematics. It concerns grouping, matching, categorizing and discriminating values. Classification can be based on a variety of attributes, including:

- Shapes
- Sizes
- Weight
- Length
- Width
- Height.

Once students learn the qualitative attributes, they should move to the quantity level. Here, they learn how to use both characteristics together for classification. This requires the general knowledge of several concepts, including *more, less, none, a few* and *many*. It includes specific number values as well—for example, 10, two sets of 10, and more.

Developing Classification

There are three sequential stages involved in classification:

1. First, you need to learn how to discriminate against the same or different values. Students may face difficulty in understanding the dichotomy of different/same and same/not so same. To clear up their confusion, the focus should be on the features of the objects being classified.
2. The identification of the criteria is based on several objects that need to be classified. Once they have made that identification, the students can categorize, group or match objects according to their instructions.
3. Consider dimensions in order to classify according to variety.

Ordering

Another basic concept of mathematics everyone should know is ordering objects. There is a specific criterion that decides how objects should be ordered.

To better understand this concept, students should begin with real-life objects. For example, they can order family members based on their age and more. Once they learn this concept using real-life objects, students should move on to numerical values. The idea of classification and order should be learned in conjunction with one another. For example, a student should know how to sort objects based on their sizes, from the smallest to the largest.

Spatial and Positional Concepts

It is vital to learn basic spatial and positional concepts before tackling more complex geometric problems. Some of these ideas include the notions of top, bottom, beside, next to, straight, center, middle, around, line, curved and more. Each of these concepts is critical to the basic understanding of mathematical theories.

Once these basic concepts are learned, students can move on to more complex ones such as angles, parallel, diagonal, intersecting, perpendicular, rotating and more. Students must learn how to positionally order objects. It is essential for sorting out, working with sets and seriating. For that, the student must understand first, second, third, before, after, last, next and more.

How to develop a basic understanding of position and space

The concepts of position and space are learned in geometry. Students need a basic knowledge of dimensional objects. After that, they should grasp the concept of two-dimensional shapes. They should understand what diagrams and illustrations mean and, after that, move on to symbolic representations.

Students should also exhibit knowledge of discriminating spatial and positional objects using one sentence. For example, "Both objects are circular" or "This is the smallest tree."

Using Measuring Tools

Every student must know the appropriate tools and their use for measuring quantities. Teachers must teach students about the measurement a particular tool is associated with.

How to develop an understanding of measuring tools

Learning about measuring tools will not be difficult if the students know why these tools are used and what their purpose is.

Students should be taught how these tools can be used in functional applications and how to use them in their daily lives.

The Most Commonly Used Tools for Measurements

Once students are familiar with the basic measurement tools, they should be allowed to use more complex and advanced tools. Some basic tools that could be modified for visually impaired students include:

Linear tools

- Rulers in a variety of sizes
- Measuring tape
- Click ruler
- Micrometer caliper
- Tape measures that have staples at the foot and notches at each inch

Liquid

- Battery-operated level indicator
- Metal spoon with a long handle that can be bent at 90 degrees
- Standard syringe
- Standard plastic measuring containers

Weight

- Scales to weigh up to two pounds
- Balance scale with trays and tactile needle to weigh liquids and tiny items

Temperature

- Thermometer for liquids
- Thermometer for air and body

Time

- Clocks and watches

The approaches mentioned above can ensure that students are familiar with basic mathematical concepts. This will help them solve complex or real-life mathematical problems.

Chapter 10: Writing Ability and Experience

You need to learn the fundamental standards of written English if you want to help your students with writing. The exam will test you on your error-detecting skills in major areas of the written English language. Therefore, you need to learn what is correct and what is incorrect in writing.

Grammar

Grammar rules are a set of socially acceptable patterns, including everything from spoken to written English. Punctuation and speech are two essential areas of grammar. Learning grammar is vital for effective communication.

How to use grammar

To use grammar, you need to understand how words and phrases are created and used in a sentence. Students should learn how to use words effectively. This will improve their ability to communicate and can prevent misunderstanding.

Homonyms

Homonyms are words that have multiple meanings. These words are spelled the same but are used in a variety of contexts and have similar pronunciations. For example, the word *scale* can be used in a variety of contexts. In rock climbing, the action of climbing up a wall is referred to as *scaling*. It is also the equipment used to weigh various objects. Also, the outer textured layer of a fish's body is referred to as *scales*.

The above example shows how one word could mean various things and be used in multiple ways. It could be used as a noun or a verb depending upon the context. Homonyms are also associated with homophones.

Homophones

Words that sound alike but are written differently are known as homophones. These words have different spellings and different meanings. The most common example is *to*, *two* and *too*. All of these words sound the same. However, they have different purposes and hence, entirely different meanings. They are not synonyms.

Homographs

Words that are spelled the same and have a different meaning are known as homographs. The context in which they are used depends upon the sentence. For example, the word *close* can be used in two ways, depending upon the sentence it is used in. For example, *close* means "to shut," as in "Close the door." On the other hand, it also means "near," as in "We sat close to each other."

Distinguishing between homonyms, homophones and homographs can be confusing. Each of these words sound and sometimes are spelled the same, but they have entirely different meanings. They cannot be interchanged. Therefore, while learning grammar, you need to ensure that you are using the right word in the proper context in a sentence.

This is especially important if you are typing a document using the computer. This is because the computer program will only check a word for its spelling. It may not identify a wrong homonym used in a sentence if the word is spelled right.

Apostrophes

There are two reasons to use apostrophes:

- To create a contraction
- To indicate possession.

Possession

The most common use of the apostrophe is to indicate possession. It is added at the end of a word to show possession. For example, *Tom's hat, Toby's shoes, Anna's scarf* and so on. Various words already end with an *s*. The rule is slightly different for such words. For example, if you want to show that Rufus owns a bicycle using an apostrophe, you will write it as *Rufus' bicycle*.

In certain cases, you can also follow the simple practice already mentioned. This means you can write it as *Rufus's bicycle*. No matter which style you choose, make sure to stick to it. However, for plural nouns that end with an *s*, you only add an apostrophe sign at the end of the word. You do not need to add another word to a noun that already ends with an *s*.

Exception

The rules are different when an apostrophe is used with the word *it*. You add *s* without an apostrophe to *it* to show possession. For example, in the sentence "This cat loves its owner," *s* is added to *it* without an apostrophe even though it indicates possession. "This building has lost its pristine novelty to time." In this example, *it* is also used to show possession.

If you add an apostrophe *s* to *it*, you create a contraction rather than indicating possession.

Contraction

As mentioned earlier, the apostrophe can be used in a variety of ways. It is used when two words are joined to create a contraction. Here, the apostrophe *s* is added in place of the missing letter or letters. For example, *can* and *not* can be written together as *can't*. *Could* and *not* can be fused to create the contraction *couldn't*. Similarly, *it* and *is* can be joined together in a contraction. The new word formed is written as *it's*.

Contractions are not encouraged in formal writing. While teaching your students the rules of English grammar, teach them what is formal and informal writing so they know when using contractions is acceptable.

Confusing Words

In the English language, there are a variety of different words that mean the same thing. However, all of them are used in a different context. Some of them are grammatically correct and some incorrect. For example, if you want to refer to a smaller amount of something, you will either use *less* or *fewer*. The choice of words used depends upon the context of the sentence. *Fewer* is used in the sentences where the objects are countable. On the contrary, *less* is used when the object cannot be quantified.

Capitalization

Capitalization is another fundamental rule of English grammar. It is the use of uppercase letters in a sentence. Words are capitalized:

- At the beginning of a sentence
- When a proper noun is mentioned
- In titles
- In acronyms
- When the pronoun *I* is used
- When an event or time period is mentioned.

The writer should capitalize words only when necessary. If a sentence is written in all uppercase letters, the writer's intent may be misunderstood. The reader will feel as if the writer is yelling.

Different writing style guides include different capitalization rules. Proper use depends to some degree upon the scenario. Therefore, be sure to stay consistent with the style throughout.

When should words be capitalized?

At the start of a sentence

Every sentence should begin with a capital letter. This rule also applies to a new sentence written within a quote. For example:

She opened the window and said, "Ah! What a wonderful day to go for a walk."

Proper nouns

Proper nouns should be capitalized. These include the names of people, things, events and places. Here are some examples:

I want to visit my sister in Denver, Colorado, this summer.

The capital of Egypt is Cairo.

I planned a romantic dinner for my wife at the base of the Eiffel Tower.

Pronoun *I*

Whether it is written at the beginning of the sentence, in the middle or the end, the pronoun *I* will always be written in the uppercase. Here are some examples:

I lost my cat.

My cousin and I are planning a trip up north.

Acronyms

When an abbreviation is formed by using the first letter of every word, an acronym is formed. Every letter is capitalized in an acronym. We come across various acronyms in our day-to-day life. Some examples include:

- *UCLA* is the acronym for the "University Of California Los Angeles."
- *AI* is the acronym for "artificial intelligence."
- *UI* is the acronym for "user interface."
- *BRB* is the acronym for "be right back."
- *ASAP* is the acronym for "as soon as possible."

Titles

Most of the words that appear in the title of a song, a book or a play are capitalized. However, there are a few exceptions. It depends upon the style guide being used.

Punctuation

Punctuation marks serve as road signs for readers. They make it easier for the author to communicate ideas. These marks specify when the reader should pause or stop while reading. They also show whether a sentence is a question or a declarative statement. Students need to understand the motive of each of the punctuation rules to understand the text better.

Punctuation at the end of a sentence

Punctuation found at the end of a sentence is referred to as end punctuation. End punctuation can be of three types.

Periods

The period marks the end of a sentence. It is added at the end of a declarative sentence. This type of punctuation does not add any emotion to the sentence. It simply implies that the statement is over.

Question marks

A question mark comes at the end of an interrogative question. These sentences pose uncertainty. The addition of a question mark indicates that the sentence is not declarative.

Exclamation marks

An exclamation mark adds a powerful emotion of excitement to a sentence. When a period is added to "let's go," it becomes a declarative sentence. However, when you add an exclamation mark to this sentence, it adds strong emotion or excitement to it.

A writer uses this punctuation mark to imply that the reader should pay attention to a particular statement. However, this punctuation mark should not be frequently used. In some cases, an exclamation mark indicates an elevated voice. Therefore, it should be used only when it is necessary.

Other common punctuation marks

Various punctuation marks are added to the beginning or middle of a sentence. These marks impart more meaning to the statement. Some of the most commonly used punctuation marks in the English language include:

Commas

The comma is one of the most commonly used punctuation marks. It is also misused often. The purpose of a comma is to indicate a pause.

Commas also separate words or word groups in a list. This punctuation mark is also added when dates, geographical locations and numbers are mentioned in a sentence. Commas are also added after an introductory phrase or word.

Oxford or serial comma

Another concept associated with the use of the comma includes the serial, or Oxford, comma. This is the comma that is added right before the conjunction near the end of a list. For example, apples, oranges, and apples is an example of using the serial comma. Notice the comma right before "and." A few writing style guides discourage the use of this comma.

Quotation marks

In some sentences, the author needs to denote someone else's words. In this case, quotation marks are used. The statement written within the quotation marks is not the author's statement. This text is written word by word as a quote from someone else or, in the case of fiction, character dialogue.

This punctuation mark can be used to separate a direct quote from the author's words. It can also be added to highlight a phrase, word or concept the reader might be unfamiliar with.

Sometimes, quotations are used around titles, articles, poems or generally shorter pieces of text. There are two types of quotation marks—double and single. In the majority of cases, double quotation marks are used. However, when there is a quote or dialogue within another quote or dialogue, the single quotation mark is used on the interior quoted material. For example,

"The other day, my teacher asked me, 'Where have you been the entire semester?' But I couldn't reply," Ryan told his therapist.

Sometimes, punctuating with quotation marks can get confusing. It can be difficult to understand where to add quotation marks while dealing with other punctuation marks in a sentence.

Apostrophes

The apostrophe has two purposes:

- To show contraction

- To show possession.

See our earlier discussion of apostrophes.

Colons

Colons are added to sentences that introduce a list. These are added to the text where the content is divided into bullet points. This punctuation mark should be used only if it does not interrupt the flow of the text.

Semicolons

Semicolons serve as speed bumps for readers as they go through a text. They are used when a long sentence is written. A semicolon pauses readers in mid-sentence so that they can make more sense of the sentence. However, semicolons do not bring the reader to a complete stop.

The primary purpose of a semicolon is to join two independent clauses. It replaces internal commas when it comes to linking clauses with a transitional expression. It ensures that the sentence does not look too long or confusing or have too many commas.

Ellipses

When a word or words are omitted from a quoted source, ellipses are added. Ellipses are three dots. They indicate missing words or someone who ended a statement by trailing off...

Parentheses

Sometimes an author needs to subtly add information to a sentence. Parentheses are used only when additional information needs to be added to a sentence. Parentheses separate additional information, written to increase readers' understanding of the subject, from the actual sentence.

Hyphens and dashes

Hyphens and dashes are two entirely different punctuation marks. The shortened version of the dash is known as a hyphen. It joins two words together. It creates a compound word when added between two words.

Dashes are used when the author wants to show the connection between two items. It is sometimes used to replace parentheses, colons or commas. Dashes impact the tone of the sentence. Therefore, they should be used only when necessary. An author should not overuse dashes because they may change the tone of the sentence.

How to Prevent Grammatical Errors

The base of a language is built over centuries. However, it keeps on evolving. Grammar serves as a system that improves the readability of a text and maintains its structure. Different languages have different sets of grammatical rules. Learning these rules is important for developing good grammar skills. This is especially important for those students whose primary language is not English.

With the advent of the internet, written and oral communication has grown. The English language has become more familiar to people from all across the world. These circumstances have made it even more important to learn the proper usage of English as the primary medium of communication.

Learning grammar and using complete sentences is vital for clear global communication. Grammatical errors affect the readability of a document as well as create faulty communication.

Chapter 11: Applying Writing Skills

Writing requires you to have a basic knowledge of English grammar. You need to know how sentences are formed. This includes the parts of speech and how they should be put together. There are eight parts of speech in the English language. We will discuss each of them in detail.

The Parts of Speech

Nouns

Words that name a place, person, thing or idea are known as nouns. There are two types of nouns: common nouns and proper nouns. Common nouns name nothing specific. These nouns could be anything from a block, school, cat, girl or a town. Proper nouns are names of a specific person, name, place, event or thing. These nouns start with capital letters. Examples include the Eiffel Tower, Dolly the cloned sheep, Ferrari and more.

Verbs

Verbs are words that show an action the subject takes or a state a subject is in. They have three forms—past, present and future.

The present tense indicates the action that is currently taking place. The past tense indicates an action that has already taken place, and the future tense shows an action that is yet to be taken. *Eat, yelled, swim, sing, drive* and *help* are a few examples of verbs.

Adjectives

A word that changes or describes a noun or verb is known as an adjective. In English grammar, adjectives offer description and details regarding a verb or a noun. These details help readers better understand what the author is trying to communicate. It helps them closely envision the context of the text.

The purpose of an adjective is to add more sensory details to a sentence. It tells the readers how something appears, smells, tastes, feels and sounds. Adjectives can also tell the quantity of a noun. Words such as *more, hundreds, quiet, noisy, cold, warm, red, tired, short* and *tall* are a few examples of adjectives.

Adverbs

Adverbs describe a verb in a sentence. They better explain how an action is taking place. In certain cases, they provide more information about verbs. Verbs are the actions that the subject performs, and adverbs explain how that particular action takes place. The majority of adverbs end in –*ly*. Some common examples of verbs include *slowly, patiently, happily, sadly* and *sleepily*.

Pronouns

Pronouns replace nouns in a sentence. With the help of pronouns, the writer does not need to repeatedly use the name of a person or object. Look at this example:

Jennifer wore Jennifer's mother's wedding dress on Jennifer's wedding day.

This sentence looks very repetitive, as *Jennifer* is used repeatedly. It can also confuse the reader. To make it more readable, the writer can use pronouns instead of some of the nouns. Once the noun is replaced with a pronoun, this sentence reads:

On her wedding day, Jennifer wore her mother's wedding dress.

By replacing some nouns with pronouns, this sentence is made easier to follow than it was before.

Conjunctions

The words that join a sentence are known as conjunctions. The part of speech that allows the author to link words, clauses or phrases in a sentence is known as a conjunction. These words serve as a tool so the writer can put a sentence together in a more elevated or sophisticated way. Short, choppy sentences affect the flow of the content. Therefore, it is important to link them together using conjunctions. In English grammar, three types of conjunctions are commonly used:

- Coordinating
- Correlative
- Subordinating.

Coordinating conjunctions

The seven most commonly used coordinating conjunctions are, *for, and, nor, but, or, yet* and *so*—the *FANBOYS*.

Correlative conjunctions

Sometimes, conjunctions appear in pairs to create a balanced sentence. The most commonly used correlative conjunctions include *both/and, either/or, not only/but, whether/or* and *neither/nor.*

To use these conjunctions correctly and effectively in a sentence, the writer must ensure that both conjunctions in the pair appear. For example:

Not only did Sarah win the beauty pageant, but she was also presented with a cash prize.

Gabriella is good at both chemistry and singing.

Subordinating conjunctions

Subordinating conjunctions are added to a sentence for a specific purpose. They form a connection between ideas by joining both dependent and independent clauses.

These relationships can be of a variety of types, including a contrast or comparison, cause and effect, or a sense of order. Some commonly used subordinating conjunctions include *that, though, if, then, because, once, since, given, provided, whereas, unless, until, although, before* and *after.*

Interjections

The part of speech that adds more feeling or emotion to a sentence is known as an interjection. The majority of the time, interjections are the exclamations that appear at the beginning or the end of a sentence. For example:

Oh dear! It is freezing cold outside.

"Ah! What a relief."

Another purpose of adding interjections to writing is to indicate a pause in the sentence. For example:

Yes! That's an amazing piece of art!

Prepositions

A preposition indicates a spatial relationship between two or more objects in a sentence. For example:

What will a cat do with a box? It will go above, below, over, under and around it.

Sentence Structure

Sentence structure shows how clauses and phrases are put together coherently. There are various types of sentences.

Complete sentences

A complete sentence contains a subject and a verb. It should reflect a complete thought. Apart from the basic sentence, these elements can also be added to create more complex and longer sentences. Two basic requirements complete a sentence:

- The subject—it tells who or what the sentence is about. In most cases, it is a noun or a pronoun.
- The verb—also known as a predicate. It indicates the action the subject takes or its state.

Every word associated with the subject is part of the complete subject. Every word associated with the verb is a part of the complete verb. Sometimes you are asked to identify complete subjects or predicates in a sentence. They are simply the noun and the verb.

Sentence fragments

A sentence fragment is also referred to as an incomplete sentence. When any of the basic elements of a complete sentence are missing, a sentence fragment is formed. The missing word can be either a noun or a verb. Sentence fragments cannot convey a complete thought or idea. For example, "Because sun" is a sentence fragment. Because the sun what? The thought behind the sentence is incomplete.

You can identify a sentence fragment by its length. You need to be very careful while trying to test a sentence for completion. In certain cases, the subject is not explicitly mentioned, as it was mentioned in the previous sentence.

Run-on sentences

A run-on sentence contains too many independent clauses linked without proper punctuation. In these types of sentences, various ideas are crammed together without punctuation marks, muddying the author's meaning. Here is an example:

Martha went to the store she went to the doctor and she went to the post office by then she was tired and hurried home for lunch.

That's a very difficult sentence to read since it lacks all punctuation. It's much easier to read the following sentence:

Martha went to the store. She went to the doctor and also to the post office. By then, she was tired and hurried home for lunch.

Note that two independent clauses shouldn't be joined by a comma, or you end up with a comma splice.

You can avoid a run-on sentence by adding commas or another punctuation mark to link one clause to another in certain cases. However, commas are not strong enough to create a connection between two independent clauses. Therefore, when added to a run-on sentence, they create a comma splice.

Comma splices should be avoided, as they affect a document's readability. Here, the writer needs to add a coordinating conjunction in the sentence to link two clauses. The author can also replace commas with semicolons to create a proper structure.

Parallelisms

Parallelism requires every verb in a sentence to be conjugated the same way. It is important for creating a balanced sentence. For example,

She ran to the store and sang a song while running.

This sentence has correct parallel structure versus

She ran to the store and singing a song while running.

Modifiers

Modifiers are adverbs and adjectives. These words or phrases provide readers with more information about the sentences' topic. They allow the author to paint a visual picture in the reader's mind.

However, it is important to use modifiers the right way. If these words or phrases are not used in the correct way, they can make a sentence very confusing. There are two types of modifier issues to avoid:

Misplaced or dangling modifiers

Modifiers make sense only when they are placed right next to the word they are supposed to modify. Otherwise, it will get very confusing for the reader to understand what these modifiers are referring to.

Split infinitives

The verb that includes *to* and *a simple form of the verb* is referred to as a split infinitive. It is always better to rewrite such sentences to ensure there is no interruption in the infinitive. The modifiers for infinitive verbs should either come before or after the verb.

Agreement

When it comes to agreement in a sentence, there are three types of common mistakes. These include:

Subject-verb agreement

This is the agreement that indicates the relationship between subjects and verbs. The verb needs to be singular if a sentence only has one subject. For plural subjects, the verb needs to be the correct plural form.

Pronoun-antecedent agreement

This agreement shows the relationship between a pronoun and an antecedent. An antecedent is a named noun. The noun is replaced with a pronoun in a sentence to eliminate confusion. According to this agreement, if the antecedent is singular, its pronoun should also be singular. If an antecedent is plural, its pronoun also needs to be plural.

The writer should also consider gender and choose a pronoun accordingly to replace the subject with a pronoun.

Consistent verb tense

The time period in which an action takes place is referred to as verb tense. There are three types of tenses: past, present and future. Similarly, there is a unique form of verbs for each of these tenses. These tenses can be perfect or continuous.

It is important to ensure that you have chosen the right verb form. It should be based on the number of people involved in the action and the period in which it is taking place.

Clauses and Phrases

What is a clause?

The building blocks of a sentence are its phrases and clauses. When put together correctly, they make a complete sentence that effectively conveys the author's message. There are a few rules that direct how phrases and clauses should be put together.

Independent clause

An independent group of words that stands as a complete sentence of its own is known as an independent clause. This clause has all the characteristics of a complete sentence. It has a subject and a verb and conveys a complete thought of its own.

Even though each of the independent clauses stands as a complete sentence of its own, various independent clauses can be linked together to create a complex sentence.

Dependent clause

A dependent clause is also referred to as a subordinate clause. It is not a complete sentence of its own. It needs to be linked to an independent clause to make sense. Just like an independent clause, a dependent clause includes a subject and a verb. However, it cannot deliver a complete thought itself. Mostly, incomplete sentences or sentence fragments are independent clauses.

Phrases

A group of words that includes a noun and a verb is referred to as a phrase. However, it does not indicate if the noun is taking an action. Phrases are put together to create clauses. When added to a clause, they produce a complete sentence.

Different Types of Sentences

Reading becomes boring when every sentence follows the same pattern and has a similar structure. It is the writer's job to make a document more interesting by using a variety of sentences. When used correctly, different types of sentences keep the readers engaged. In English grammar, there are four types of sentences:

Simple sentences

The most basic form of sentences is simple sentences. These include nothing other than an independent clause. For example:

I like cake.

Compound sentences

There is more than one clause in a complex sentence. These clauses are independent and linked together by coordinating conjunctions. Commas and semicolons also frequently appear in such sentences.

I like cake, but Joanna prefers cookies.

Complex sentences

A complex clause includes one independent clause and one or more dependent clauses. It is more complex than the compound sentence.

Although I went to school today, I left at noon for a doctor's appointment.

Compound-complex sentences

Compound complex sentences are the most diverse type of sentences. They include various independent clauses. These sentences have at least one dependent clause.

Active Voice vs. Passive Voice

Two types of voices appear in an author's writing: active voice and passive voice. Sentences written in the active voice are more powerful. They are easier to understand. Most sentences should be in the active voice.

Passive voice is more poetic than active voice. When used unnecessarily in a piece of writing, passive voice sentences may confuse the reader.

Active-voice sentences

A sentence in which the subject actively performs an action is referred to as an active voice sentence. You can write it in the present, past or future tense. No matter where the action takes place, the subject has to directly perform it. For example:

We are going to watch the football game.

Passive-voice sentences

The sentences in which the subject does not actively perform an action are passive voice sentences. The subject passively receives the action. Such sentences confuse the reader if they appear frequently. It becomes hard for readers to identify who did what and when.

The football game is going to be watched by us.

Spelling

Having strong spelling skills is important for effective communication. With technology, we have become used to automatic spellcheck tools. However, you need to spell correctly if you want to develop excellent writing skills. It is also very important for the identification of words.

Teachers must understand the importance of spelling if they want to identify spelling mistakes. One of the best ways to learn spelling and vocabulary is to use a dictionary. You can look for the words you are confused about and search for their correct spellings.

To become a paraprofessional teacher, you need to learn the basic rules for turning singular words into plural and vice versa. You should also be familiar with spelling conventions and exceptions.

Chapter 12: Editing Written Documents

Once you learn how to put ideas on a piece of paper correctly, it is time to apply what you have learned. You need to know how to guide your students in the right direction. The first step is to encourage them to use the resources available to them. That includes what you teach them and the use of a dictionary. Motivate them to become independent writers who do not require your constant help. Use a step-by-step approach to teach your students how to write.

Writing Instructions

Today, writing instructions are far different from what they were a decade ago. Teachers showing students how to write first used to start with a topic and due date. Only a few instructions were provided. This trend has changed with the advent of technology. Today, a piece of writing is judged on a specific set of standards

Instead of simply grading the text, the instructor needs to provide students with useful suggestions for improvement. Today, writing instructions have a structure and a method that guide the student in each step of the writing process.

How Writing Lessons Should Be Structured

Most schools today conduct writing workshops to teach instructors how to format a lesson structure. This structure includes a brief lesson where the teacher concisely explains each aspect of writing. Once the students have the necessary instructions, they are asked to work on an individual or group writing assignment.

To encourage students to perform their best, teachers ask them to share their work with the rest of the class. This encourages them to put in their maximum effort and helps other students learn from their classmates.

Writing Structure Guidelines

According to research, students write better when they are provided with detailed written instructions instead of a blank piece of paper. Different writing techniques require to be written in a specific format. Each of them follows a different structure. One of the most commonly used formats is the five-paragraph essay. This form of writing is divided into five paragraphs:

- The first paragraph includes the introduction or thesis statement.

- The second paragraph presents the first point and its details.

- The third paragraph presents the second point and discusses it in detail.

- The fourth paragraph presents the third point and discusses its details.

- The fifth paragraph concludes the essay.

The Writing Process

Whether it is a group or individual assignment, students have to follow the same process while writing. There is a specific purpose behind each part of the process. You need to keep up with your students' progress at each stage. This way, you will be able to guide them better. The following are some of the most important parts of the writing process:

1. Prewriting

Planning and outlining an essay is critical to good writing. Whether the students are writing an essay, story, play or another form of written material, prewriting activities prepare them to write. These activities include:

Brainstorming

The first part of the prewriting process should always be brainstorming. Students should be encouraged to brainstorm ideas they can include in their essays. They should write each of these points to create an outline for the content. This will help them figure out which points they need to cover.

Brainstorming is the part of the prewriting process in which the writer simply writes down what comes to mind. This vague outline is given a proper structure when the writer plans out the essay's structure. The brainstormed ideas serve as a guide for the writer when crafting the essay.

Planning

Once writers have brainstormed the ideas to include in their essay, they need to create a proper plan. Having a solid plan makes the writing process easier. The writer has a script to adhere to and is clear about the purpose of the writing. Writing important points down ahead of time ensures writers do not miss any important details they have planned to add to the essay.

There is no specific structure to follow when it comes to planning out an essay. Writers should create one that suits them and is easy to follow. For some students, a list-type format works, whereas others rely on a visual style. The most commonly followed format is the five-paragraph structure discussed above.

2. Writing the first draft

In this step, the writer follows the outline during the writing process. Since it is the first draft, it is okay if the document is not perfectly presented. The student has room to make improvements in the second draft.

Research has revealed that students write better if they are not under pressure to strive for perfection in the first draft. The principal purpose of this step is to put the brainstormed ideas in writing.

Allow students to make and learn from their mistakes. Give them extra time to make corrections when they are done writing. While checking the first draft, point out mistakes using a pencil. This step will not overwhelm the students, and they will feel more in control of their writing abilities. This step will pave the way for effective editing and revising.

3. Revising

Revising does not include fixing spelling errors or grammar or punctuation. In this step, students simply need to review an essay to see whether the message is clear. If not, they should opt for a better way to organize the information. They should add or delete the words, phrases, concepts or ideas that make no sense. They should find the best way to communicate what they want to say.

4. Editing

In this step, students need to look for spelling, grammatical, punctuation, capitalization and usage errors. They should fix the errors they come across while going through the piece. Teachers should encourage students to read their writing assignments carefully. Encourage them to take their time to read and fix their assignments.

Understand that editing your own piece of writing is more challenging than pointing out flaws in somebody else's work. Help the students who find this process difficult and involve them in the editing process. You can ask them questions like, "Is this sentence complete?" and more.

5. Publishing

In a classroom, publishing means submitting the final draft of the assignment to the teacher. The submission of the final draft indicates that the writer is finished with the writing process.

What is the writing purpose?

Every author has an intent or a purpose behind each writing project. No matter which type of written material a student has been asked to produce, he or she should write with a purpose. Sometimes, there is more than one purpose behind the written piece. The writer should always keep this intent in mind. This will keep an author focused on the topic, so he or she does not drift away from the purpose.

The document's structure depends upon the writer's goal. The student must choose the structure that goes with the writing task at hand. For example, the structure of a literature review is going to be different from the format of a business email.

Different type of writer's purpose

There are four types of purpose:

- To entertain
- To persuade
- To explain
- To inform

The teacher decides the purpose of writing and mentions it in the instructions. For example, "Write an informative essay about the attack on the Capitol in 2020." However, in other cases, students need to determine the purpose of their writing assignments. In such cases, the writer decides whether the writing is going to be persuasive or informative. They have to decide whether they want to explain the event or how it could have been prevented. They can even write an entertaining piece sharing a humorous take on the events.

In most cases, the teacher provides students with a purpose. However, these instructions could be vague. It could be the teacher's way to test students' understanding of the topic. In such cases, the students need to determine the purpose of the writing and decide the approach to take for the topic at hand.

Forms and Modes of Writing

A piece of text can be written to serve a variety of purposes. Similarly, various forms and modes of writing ensure effective communication of the writer's ideas. Each of these modes serves a different purpose and sets a different tone for the written piece. Some of the most commonly used writing modes include:

Descriptive

Descriptive writing creates a mental image in the reader's mind with the effective use of imagery. This form of writing takes readers on a journey as they read. Painting a visual picture with words hooks the reader. These types of pieces are written with carefully selected words. These words appeal to the basic human senses.

Persuasive

In the persuasive form of essay writing, students are asked to convince the reader of an idea they may or may not agree with. For that, the writer needs to present powerful, convincing arguments and evidence to support these arguments. They should convince their audience that the argument is accurate and persuade them to join their position.

Narrative

Narratives are also referred to as stories. In this mode of writing, the teacher asks a student to tell a story to the audience. This story can be written in the first, second or third person. It is up to the writer whether to write the story as a personal experience or create a character to narrate the story.

Mostly, the purpose of narrative essays is to inform. However, these can also share insights or a lesson regarding the subject of the narrative.

Argumentative

Just like persuasive writing, argumentative essays also present an argument that may or may not be widely accepted. No matter what the argument is, the writer must provide evidence to prove the claim is accurate.

The purpose of an argumentative piece is to get a reader to accept the validity of the writer's argument. Even if readers disagree with the argument, they should be convinced that the presented point deserves consideration.

Letters

Formal or informal correspondence between two individuals is referred to as a letter. This mode of writing is often personal. It is intended for one receiver or a small audience group. In this form of writing, students communicate their thoughts less formally than in an essay.

Chapter 13: Types of Writing

The purpose of writing is to effectively convey a concept or thought to readers. The choice of words is important. There are several kinds of words that confuse readers:

Jargon

Jargon consists of technical words or phrases specific to a particular discipline or profession.

When to use jargon

You can use jargon as long as you are certain that your readers are familiar with the technical terms you are using in your essay.

Suppose you are writing to doctors. You can use medical terms and medical jargon in your essay. However, laypeople may not understand those terms if they read the document. This means you should never use medical jargon beyond those who belong to the medical profession. The same applies to any other type of jargon.

Slang

Slang consists of words that do not belong in formal English. These are invented and used only by a particular group of people.

When to use slang

There is usually no place for slang in professional or academic writing. However, there are exceptions. A writer can use slang when presenting a sociolinguistic study to readers, but this form of language should not be used in a casual response for an online class discussion. Apart from slang, other forms of abbreviated communication should also be avoided in formal writing.

Examples of slang include *y'all*, *yo*, *shook*, *salty* and more. Such language should be limited to texting or personal social media use.

Outdated Words

Outdated words and phrases also affect the quality of a text. For example, *dial the number*. We live in a technology-driven world where everyone owns a cell phone. No one uses a regular telephone anymore. Therefore, this phrase will only confuse readers.

Be as straightforward as you can in your writing. Euphemisms are not always appropriate. Decide on the level of formality you are striving for before you begin writing, and then make sure you stick to that level throughout your essay.

You should omit both jargon and slang from your writing to effectively convey your message. Use them only if you are addressing a particular audience or your purpose calls for it.

How to Control Wordiness

Sometimes writers use too many words in a sentence. As a result, readers cannot understand the message. Most of the time, these extra words do not even add any value to the sentence.

Cluttered sentences can be easily managed. Just eliminate the ideas and words that repeat in a sentence.

Removing repeated ideas

Presenting one idea in two ways in the same sentence is not ideal. It causes wordiness and confuses readers. However, if you are providing definitions in a sentence, you can state an idea one time.

To eliminate repeated ideas from a sentence, writers need to read the text and think about how to present the sentence concisely. They need to identify the repetitive phrases that add wordiness. By removing repetitive ideas, they can balance the sentence and make it easier to read and understand.

Let's learn this concept with the help of an example:

Use very razor-sharp scissors with spiky edges to cut the piece of cloth in half.

"Razor-sharp" and "spiky edges" are repetitive. This sentence can be rewritten as,

Use a sharp pair of scissors to cut the piece of cloth in half.

Removing repeated words

The words in a sentence that do not carry meaning should be eliminated. Shorter, concise and straightforward sentences are easier to read and understand. Repetition adds wordiness to a sentence and makes it confusing. By removing the unneeded words, you make a sentence concise and easy to comprehend.

Let's learn this concept with the help of an example:

The girl who did my makeup is a very talented and brilliant girl.

This sentence can be rewritten as:

The girl who did my makeup is very talented and brilliant.

Notice that the word *girl* has been eliminated once in the second sentence as there is no need to mention the word twice.

Removing unneeded words

Unneeded words that do not particularly add value to a sentence should be avoided. These words make the sentence long and confusing for readers. The thoughts presented in such sentences are often easily forgotten. Therefore, unnecessary words should either be reworded or removed from a sentence.

For example,

Doris has the skill to make the fluffiest butter cakes.

There is no need for "has the skill." This sentence can be rewritten as:

Doris makes the fluffiest butter cakes.

Be Straightforward

Pretentious language, euphemisms, flowery words and double-talk overwhelm readers. These choices make it difficult for an author to communicate effectively. Some misdirected techniques that make a document difficult to understand include:

Flowery or pretentious language

When an author chooses a very ornate, poetic, elaborate way to communicate with readers, the language used is flowery and pretentious. This choice of words confuses the reader and adds wordiness to a plain sentence. Avoid sentences with too many complicated phrases and words in formal writing. The intent behind using this type of language is often to appear more skillful.

For example:

I am delighted beyond words to receive the invitation to your family dinner. I would love to spend this feast night at your place. However, I already have a commitment that I cannot miss.

This sentence could be written in simple words as:

Thanks for inviting me to your family's dinner. I won't be able to attend as I already have another commitment.

Euphemisms

Euphemisms are a way to state an offensive or arguable expression in a less offensive or pleasant way. Such choice of words is often discouraged in professional or academic writing because such expressions may not directly convey the author's message.

For example,

My brother is physically challenged.

This sentence can be straightforwardly written as

My brother is a quadriplegic.

Choose an Appropriate Formality Level

Every writer should decide a document's level of formality before beginning to write. Sometimes authors do not maintain the same level of formality all throughout a document. This mistake confuses readers. Therefore, writers should decide on a specific formality level in the beginning and stick to it all the way through.

Formality levels vary from situation to situation, subject to subject, and topic to topic. The writer should choose the formality level that makes it easier for the readers to identify the meaning. The purpose of writing should drive the choice of formality level, as well as the subject and audience. For example, if you are writing about a couple of friends texting each other about going bowling, the level of formality should be low. However, if the text is regarding the death of a mutual friend, the formality level should be high.

Keep It Concise

The best way to convey your thoughts is to use precise wording because it helps you accurately relay ideas to your readers. There are various strategies to follow if you cannot communicate your thoughts in a minimum number of words. You can focus on denotation and connotation. You can use figurative language with concrete words to accurately send your message. Using specific words to directly state facts also helps. You should also avoid misused or cliché words or phrases.

Focus on Denotation and Connotation

In the English language, various words have the same meaning. For example, *laid-back* and *lackadaisical* have the same meaning, which is "slow-moving." When readers come across *laid-back* in a sentence, they easily understand what the writer is trying to say. However, if the word is replaced by *lackadaisical*, readers may not understand so clearly.

The direct definition of a word is known as its denotation. The emotional meaning or feeling of a particular word is its connotation.

For example:

- Thrilled
- Nervous
- Anxious.

The apparent meaning of each of these words is stirred-up emotions. In most cases, each of these words is considered a synonym of the other. This means the denotations of the above words are the same. Now let's look at their connotations.

The word *thrilled* is often used positively. The word *nervous* connotes an upset state of mind. Similarly, the word *anxious* connotes loss of control. While choosing a word, authors should consider its denotation first. If it matches their intent, authors should choose the connotation of the word to make the document's word usage more varied.

Add Concrete Words

Using specific and concrete words makes text more interesting and clear. On the other hand, abstract words make information hard to grasp.

Use Figurative Language

The best way to make writing more interesting is to use language tools. These tools include idioms, analogies, alliteration, hyperbole, onomatopoeia, personification, metaphors and similes.

Use Clichés Sparingly

Clichés, such as "Time heals all wounds," are popular phrases that everyone can relate to. Because of their popularity, they are often used in writing. However, over time they become uninteresting. Readers look for innovation and originality in a document. Adding overworked phrases makes a piece of writing uninteresting. To avoid clichés in formal writing, replace those phrases with plain language.

Chapter 14: Compose Essays, Narratives And Letters

Descriptive Essays

Essays that vividly describe a particular subject are referred to as descriptive. Apart from an essay, a descriptive piece of writing could be anything from an article, book report, travelogue, memoir or newspaper article.

Why are descriptive essays written?

Descriptive essays provide readers with a strong understanding of a subject. This form of writing fleshes out a topic using figurative language and solid details.

After reading a descriptive essay, the reader has a clear picture of the topic. A descriptive essay can be about anything, including a historical event or personal experience, a piece of art or a geographic location.

How is a descriptive essay written?

Organization, the use of sensory language and concrete details are a few of the most important characteristics of a descriptive essay. This kind of writing is fact-based. The writer rarely shares an opinion in this form of writing.

To write a descriptive essay, you need to follow a step-by-step procedure. These steps include:

Choosing the topic

While writing a descriptive essay, you should choose a specific topic. The purpose of the essay is decided before anything else. Once the your purpose is apparent, create an outline. Summarize the key ideas of the essay in the thesis statement.

The thesis statement is fact based. It does not reflect your point of view. It is focused on your purpose and makes your intent clear to readers.

Collect information

A descriptive essay should be full of details. These include everything from names to dates, background information, physical characteristics and more. Sensory information is an important feature of descriptive writing. Choose words that evoke different feelings and create an image in the minds of your audience.

The details added to descriptive essays should be well researched. They should be based on facts rather than opinions. Collect important facts before writing a descriptive essay and add those to specific categories of information. This will make it easier to remember every detail, and you can pull it up when needed.

Create an outline

Organization is an important characteristic of descriptive writing. Create an outline and stick to it until the essay ends. Write down the focal points of an essay and group them to incorporate them into body paragraphs when needed. Each of these paragraphs is a subcategory of the principal topic.

Writing the introduction

A good descriptive essay begins with an engaging introductory paragraph. It serves as a road map for the entire essay. One way to write the introductory paragraph of a descriptive essay is to start with a question. This trick "hooks" readers.

Once you have written the hook, work toward developing the context or topic the essay is going to cover. Place the thesis statement at the end of the introductory paragraph to make the most impact.

Writing body paragraphs

Each body paragraph tackles a different aspect of the major topic. It should start with a topic sentence that may or may not state the dominant idea the paragraph has to present. Write this sentence to anchor the reader's attention. It should clearly state what the readers should expect from the paragraph.

While writing body paragraphs, be specific. Present information in a way that does not overwhelm the readers. You can also use subheadings and bullet points to more clearly develop your ideas.

Writing the conclusion

The conclusion reiterates the main ideas presented in the introductory paragraph. It also presents key details stated in the body paragraphs. Additional information should never be introduced in the concluding paragraph.

Enlivening language used in the essay

Before submitting the final draft, go through it and look for sentences that can be improved with the addition of sensory details. Add these details to enhance the idea you are trying to convey.

Look for opportunities to tell a story to evoke readers' senses. Choose the right literary tools to ensure that your descriptive essay lives in your audience's mind long after they are done reading.

Narratives

A narrative is a combination of personal story-telling and academic argument. In a narrative, the writer shares universal lessons with readers through his or her unique experiences. This form of writing exhibits some characteristics of a descriptive essay. It also focuses on details that truly immerse readers into the author's experience.

Some important features of narratives include:

- They are nonfiction.
- They are often autobiographical.
- They are not always strictly fact-based.

How narratives differ from short stories

Narratives usually include dramatic descriptions. Similar to short stories, they also include a plot, characters and dialogue. Due to the overlap of these structural elements, readers often confuse narrative writing with short stories. However, there are a few distinguishing features that set narratives apart from short stories. Some of them include:

A narrative presents a point or argument

The purpose of a narrative is to put forth an argument or a point. The writer weaves the entire essay around this idea. Narratives are focused on making a point, whereas short stories are focused on plot.

A narrative is conclusive

A narrative completely concludes the topic and ensures there are no questions left unanswered. Short stories do not always end so conclusively.

First person

Narratives are often written in first person.

Structure

Narratives are organized into an introductory paragraph, body paragraphs and conclusion. On the other hand, short stories do not always follow a specific format.

The format of a narrative

The structure of a narrative includes:

Introduction

The introductory paragraph presents the narrative's theme. It states the fundamental idea of the topic but does not give away too much information.

Body paragraphs

The author develops his or her argument in the body paragraphs. These paragraphs describe events and scenes that the writer experienced. Character development may also take place in body paragraphs through dialogue.

Conclusion

A narrative ends with a conclusion that provides readers with a brief reflection of what they have learned in the preceding paragraphs. It touches back on the key points discussed in the piece of writing.

Popular topics of narratives

In a narrative, the author shares a personal experience. The nature of such essays sets them apart from the other genres of writing. There are a variety of topics that can be covered in these essays. While writing a narrative, the author needs to present readers with a point or argument and weave the essay around that point.

Some common topics for narratives include:

- A failure
- How you overcame adversity
- How a life experience changed you
- Something you experienced for the first time
- An experience you had in a relationship and what it taught you
- An incident that affected your childhood
- A memorable place you visited and how visiting it changed you.

Letters

We live in a technology-driven world where letter writing has become something of a lost art. Email and text messages have replaced letters. However, for business communication, letters still hold a lot of value.

Types of letters

There are two types of letters: formal and informal.

How to write formal letters

A formal letter should begin with the address of the writer written on the top right corner of the page. The date should be added below the writer's address. On the left-hand side, below the writer's address and date, the recipient's name and address are added.

The letter is opened with Dear Sir/Dear Madam, etc. The opening sentence should clearly explain its purpose. Each paragraph of the letter should discuss a specific point. The formality level and choice of words should be high. Abbreviations, slang and contractions should be avoided.

In the concluding paragraph, the writer explains what he or she is asking for. The letter ends with a formal note, such as *Sincerely*.

How to write an informal letter

Similar to all other genres of writing, informal letters should begin with proper planning. The first step is to sketch an outline to stick to throughout the writing. This outline should be concise and should not include minute details. Consider the following points while creating an outline for an informal letter:

- The name and addresses of the recipient or recipients
- The purpose of the letter and the fundamental idea you want to communicate
- The points you will discuss in each of the body paragraphs.

An informal letter opens with a greeting. The choice of words depends upon the formality of the relationship. If you are addressing an acquaintance, you can use *Dear* or *Hi*.

The opening greeting is followed by a general opening sentence. Most of the time, *How are you?* Or *I hope you are doing great* is used.

After the general opening sentence, state the reason for writing. An open and friendly tone is used in informal letters. Unlike formal letters, informal letters are rather relaxed.

The choice of closing depends upon the level of formality between the writer and recipient. Some commonly used examples include *Love* and *Thanks*.

Chapter 15: Writing Guidelines

Learning grammar rules can sometimes be boring. However, teachers should think of ways to make grammar lessons more interesting. With technology, the approach to teaching grammar has changed. Worksheets used to be considered the best way to learn grammar rules. However, this approach has been replaced with task-based learning. This approach teaches students much more than just grammar rules. They also get to learn why these grammar rules are important.

For example, if you introduce your students to adverbs, teach them how to use them in actual life. This makes grammar lessons more interesting.

Grammar Tools Students Should be Introduced To

There are various grammar tools teachers can introduce to students to make grammar lessons more interesting and exciting for them. Some of these tools include:

Visual aids

The best way to teach students the proper use of grammar is through visual aids. These tools include:

Photos

The task-based learning approach uses visual imagery to make grammar lessons more interesting and memorable. You can assign students a topic and ask them to bring in a couple of related photos. Provide them with proper instructions so that they know what they are supposed to do. These pictures can be of anything, such as images of their favorite activity, pets or siblings. Display these photos for the class.

Ask the students to interpret the images and identify the subject, object, action, noun or verbs in the picture. For example, if it is a picture of a person baking a cake, you can ask the student which part of speech *baking* is. If it is a picture of a cat playing with a ball of yarn, ask the student to identify nouns in the picture. Make the most of this activity by ensuring that the students clearly understand all parts of speech by the end of the exercise.

If you are dealing with older students, you can ask them to write a descriptive essay or short story about the photo.

Sentence diagrams

Apart from task-based learning, various other visual grammar tools make learning a fun and engaging experience for the students. Sentence diagrams make it easier for students to learn the most important components of speech.

These diagrams are exceptionally useful, as they break a sentence into different parts of speech. Most sentence diagrams follow the same basic formula:

Subject + verb + direct object

However, there are variations. These variations cover other parts of speech, including adverbs and adjectives. By breaking down a sentence into a diagram on the board, you make it easier for the students to identify each part of speech. You should also ask them to note the diagram in their journals or memorize the basic formula. These rules will stay with them for years to come.

Game of opposites

If you are teaching your students the concept of synonyms and antonyms, the game of opposites can be of great help. This teaching approach kills two birds with one stone. It not only helps students learn opposites of a word, but it also helps them develop an extensive vocabulary.

In this game, write a word on the board and asks students to write its opposite. In various cases, there will be more than one appropriate answer. You can also ask students to write as many synonyms of a word as possible. This will widen their vocabulary. For example, if you write *light* on the board, the students will write *heavy* as its synonym.

Classroom activities

When teaching grammar, physical movement is not as popular as using visual aids. However, by combining some type of movement with a new concept, you can ensure that students better retain this information. Various classroom activities help students learn a new grammatical concept. Some of these activities include:

Conjugation bee

A conjugation bee is very similar to a spelling bee. This helps students better grasp the concept of irregular verbs. There is no specific set of rules for teaching irregular verbs. They are tricky and do not follow basic grammar rules. Conjugation bee exercises make it easier to learn these verbs. This exercise involves:

- Calling out the irregular verb or verb tense in a sentence.

- Asking the student to identify the verb in a sentence. Once they successfully do this, ask them to tell its past tense. For example, the past tense of *make* is *made*.
- If the answer is incorrect, the student is out of the game.
- The game continues until there is only one student left.

Grammar potato

Grammar potato is an interesting and fun classroom activity that keeps students on their toes. It engages all students and ensures that everyone learns while having a good time. The idea behind this game is very simple. All you need to do is to choose a grammar topic, for example, nouns. Announce the topic and provide students with an example, like "car." Pass on the potato in the classroom. The student with the potato has to say the name of a noun within the provided time limit.

You can make this competition even more interesting by asking the students to come up with a noun that begins with the last letter of the previous response. For example, the word *car* could be followed by *rat,* followed by a word that starts with *T,* such as *table.*

Modifiers

A modifier is the part of speech that changes the other words in a sentence. It can be a phrase or a clause. In the majority of the cases, it is an adverb or an adjective. Adjectives change nouns. Adverbs modify verbs. Modifiers as adverbs also change adjectives and other adverbs.

Types of modifier problems

There are three types of modifier problems:

Misplaced modifiers

When a modifier is in the wrong place in a sentence, it is referred to as a misplaced modifier. Simple modifiers are misplaced the most. These modifiers include *just, only, barely* and *nearly.* For example:

She barely ran fifty yards.

If the meaning of the sentence is that she just made it to fifty yards, then the correct form of this sentence is

She ran barely fifty yards.

Students should learn where the modifier needs to be correctly placed in a sentence because its placement can completely change a sentence's meaning.

Dangling modifiers

When a sentence starts with a modifier, it is important to ensure that it modifies the next part of the sentence. This modifier can be a word, a phrase or a clause. A modifier is referred to as a dangling modifier if it incorrectly modifies the other parts of the sentence or paragraph. This usually happens when a sentence begins with a participial phrase. For example,

Updating Windows every few weeks, the laptop seemed to run faster.

This sentence could be rewritten as:

The laptop seems to run faster when Windows is updated every few weeks.

Squinting modifiers

A squinting modifier is another problem that frequently occurs. The issue arises when the adverb pops up almost anywhere in a sentence. Structurally, such adverbs may fit well in the sentence. However, their meaning might be ambiguous or obscure. For example,

Students who participate in extracurricular activities <u>often</u> stay ahead of their peers.

In the sentence above, it is hard to tell whether students frequently participate in extracurricular or they can frequently perform better than their peers by participating in these activities. In this sentence, *often* is the squinting modifier. It is hard to tell which part of the sentence it is referring to. We can improve this sentence by placing the adverb somewhere else:

Students who <u>often</u> participate in extracurricular activities stay ahead of their peers

Shifts in Verb Tense

Tense shifts occur when a writer switches from one tense to another in an essay, story, paragraph or even the same sentence. In certain cases, this shift is necessary. However, accidental shifts impact the structure of a sentence. These shifts take place when the writer loses focus.

This usually happens when the writer writes a story in third person. The author begins the story in the past and then accidentally switches to the present tense. In certain cases, the writer loses track of tense and keeps shifting back and forth.

To avoid this issue, choose one tense and stay consistent with it throughout the piece. If it is a narrative or you are describing an event that took place a long time ago, make sure you choose the past tense. To pull the reader into the story, writers often use the present tense. This trick works only if it is done correctly.

Pronoun Clarity

There are several types of pronoun issues. Sometimes, the problem arises when the pronoun cannot specify which particular person or a thing a sentence is referring to. For example,

Jenna was looking for <u>her</u> lost earring with Claire in <u>her</u> car. Suddenly, <u>she</u> started crying.

In this sentence, it is difficult to tell whose car the writer is referring to and who cried. The writer can rewrite the sentence in the following way to make it clearer:

Jenna was looking for her lost earring in Claire's car. Suddenly, Jenna started crying.

If pronouns are unclear, it indicates there are various competing nouns in a sentence. If that happens, the best approach is to switch back to a noun.

This confusion is also caused when the writer unintentionally switches the pronoun's person. For example,

Aaron emailed exam guidelines to the students a month in advance because he wanted everyone to come prepared for the finals. However, <u>you</u> forgot to mention the date of the exam.

In this example, the writer switches from *he* to *you*. In the first sentence, the author refers to Aaron in the third person and switches to the second person in the next sentence. This paragraph should be rewritten as:

Aaron emailed exam guidelines to the students a month in advance because he wanted everyone to come prepared for the finals. However, <u>he</u> forgot to mention the date of the exam.

Sometimes, the writer confuses quantities. This also results in pronoun confusion. For example,

The extra bag of potatoes arrived today. We have already started using <u>them</u>.

The correct form of this sentence is:

The extra bag of potatoes arrived today. We have already started using <u>it</u>.

Test 1: Reading Questions

Carefully read the passages below and answer the questions at the end of each passage.

Passage 1: The history of poaching and its impacts. (For questions 1 through 5)

According to law, poaching is the illegal trapping, shooting or taking of game, fish or plants from private property. It is a crime, as it poses serious threats to various species of wild animals worldwide. Poaching is banned in most countries, as it contributes to the loss of biodiversity.

Most poaching was performed for subsistence purposes until the start of the twentieth century. Impoverished peasants used to hunt for fish and game to feed their families. However, at the beginning of the twentieth century, European feudal landowners claimed their right to hunt on the properties they owned. This was when poaching became a crime. The punishment for this crime was imprisonment.

Special laws protected the forested countryside. These rules prevented deer and boar hunting. Laws were passed in the seventeenth and eighteenth centuries to give only landowners and their families the right to hunt and shoot wild animals. Gamekeepers were also hired to protect the wildlife that resided on these privately held lands.

These laws made subsistence poaching a more specialized activity in the eighteenth and nineteenth centuries. As a result, organized poachers used to get into fights with gamekeepers. Intruders were kept away from properties with the help of spring guns and mantraps hidden in the underbrush.

Today, poaching as a sport has been banned. However, animals are also often hunted for commercial profit, both legally and illegally. Several species have gone extinct because of poaching. It is high time for the government to take stricter action to save wildlife from unregulated hunting by sportsmen and poachers.

(1) What is the primary purpose of this passage?

(A) It explains what poaching is and how it impacts wildlife.

(B) It shows poaching is an entertaining sport.

(C) It shows that poaching results in the extinction of animals.

(D) It explains why laws against poaching are inadequate.

(2) Identify the topic sentence in the second paragraph.

(A) Most poaching was performed for subsistence purposes until the start of the twentieth century

(B) Impoverished peasants used to hunt fish and game to feed their families.

(C) However, at the beginning of the twentieth century, European feudal landowners claimed their right to hunt on the properties they owned.

(D) The punishment for this crime was imprisonment.

(3) Identify the supporting ideas in the third paragraph.

(A) Special laws protected the forested countryside

(B) These rules prevented deer and boar hunting.

(C) Laws were passed in the seventeenth and eighteenth centuries to give only landowners and their families the right to hunt and shoot wild animals

(D) Both B and C.

(4) "These laws made subsistence poaching a more specialized activity in the eighteenth and nineteenth centuries." This sentence is...

(A) A fact

(B) An opinion

(C) A universal truth

(D) Both A and B

(5) "It is high time for the government to take stricter action to save wildlife from unregulated hunting by sportsmen and poachers." What is the author's purpose in this sentence?

(A) To entertain

(B) To describe

(C) To persuade

(D) To inform

Passage 2: Why environmental sustainability is important. (For questions 6 through 10)

Environmental pollution and degradation are some of the biggest issues mankind is facing at present. With the rise in population, environmental pollution has also escalated. People are becoming more concerned about the environment than ever before. There is no part of this planet that has remained untouched by the impact of human activities.

Natural resources are under great constraint due to an increase in per capita consumption and human pollution. Apart from damage to the land, air and water quality has also been affected due to increased industrialization, urbanization and modern agricultural practices. This indicates that human activity is not only overexploiting natural resources but also contaminating them with toxic chemicals. These activities are making the survival of future generations difficult. According to the USDA (United States Development Authority) and the OECD (Organization for Economic Cooperation and Development), the increase in greenhouse gas emissions is negatively impacting the earth.

As a consequence, the global temperature is expected to rise by 02°C in 2050. This temperature rise will have a negative impact on the environment and will escalate the rate at which climate change is taking place. With a rise in global warming, glacier and polar ice is melting two to three times faster than ever before. According to research, this planet is experiencing one of the biggest phases of biodiversity loss in its history.

If these practices continue, humankind might have to prepare itself for unpredictable and unforeseen consequences. According to the United Nations, human activity has caused various plants and animal species to go extinct and put various other species at the risk of extinction. Today, this risk is a hundred times higher than the natural rate of extinction, and it is going to be even higher in the future. It is predicted that coral reefs will be completely wiped out very soon. This will cause various other species that depend upon these reefs to go extinct as well.

(6) Identify the topic sentence in the first paragraph.

(A) Environmental pollution and degradation are some of the biggest issues mankind is facing at present.

(B) People are becoming more concerned about the environment than ever before.

(C) There is no part of this planet that has remained untouched by the impact of human activities.

(D) All of the above.

(7) What is the main idea of the second paragraph?

(A) Human activity is causing the depletion of natural resources.

(B) The global population is rising with every passing day.

(C) Human activity is causing animal extinction.

(D) All of the above.

(8) "According to the USDA (United States Development Authority) and the OECD (Organization for Economic Cooperation and Development), the increase in emission of greenhouse gases is negatively impacting the earth." This sentence is...

(A) A fact

(B) An opinion

(C) A universal truth

(D) Both A and B

(9) What is the author's intent behind writing this passage?

(A) To entertain

(B) To describe

(C) To educate

(D) To inform

(10) What is the author's point of view in this passage?

(A) First person

(B) Second person

(C) Third person

(D) None of the above

Passage 3: What is causing a rise in the use of coupons? (For questions 11 through 15)

The World Wide Web has become one of the world's largest marketplaces, all because of the advent of technology. Whether big or small, almost every business has an online representation in the form of a website or social media pages. This has caused market competition to rise. Every business is trying to attract more customers by using a variety of tricks and techniques. One of the best techniques to boost sales is to launch discount coupons.

Coupon marketing is not new. Businesses have been engaging customers through coupon marketing campaigns for over a hundred years. Coca-Cola launched the first coupon in 1887. Since then, hundreds of companies have jumped on the bandwagon and introduced their customers to physical coupons. After the digitalization of the entire world, physical coupons have been replaced by digital coupons. Today, it is even easier to access coupons. Most of these coupons can be found in your mailbox or on websites dedicated to coupon distribution.

Coupon marketing benefits both the business and its customers. It helps customers save money. And it helps businesses attract more customers and hook them with products and services. It is an ideal strategy for these businesses to market their products and stay ahead of their competitors.

According to surveys, more consumers are redeeming digital coupons than ever before. The reason behind this increase in coupon redemption is inflation and a rise in the rate of unemployment. Global economic instability and a rise in population is another important factor causing consumers to look for every opportunity to save money. That is what digital coupons offer them.

From clothing to groceries to medical bills, coupons save customers a big percentage of money if used the right way. Celebrities like Lady Gaga and Kourtney Kardashian have been spotted using coupons. You should give couponing a try as well.

(11) In the first paragraph, when does the author introduce the passage's main idea?

(A) In the first sentence

(B) In the last sentence

(C) In the third sentence

(D) None of the above

(12) Identify the fact in the second paragraph.

(A) Coupon marketing is not new.

(B) Businesses have been engaging customers through coupon marketing campaigns for over a hundred years.

(C) The first coupon was launched by Coca-Cola in 1887.

(D) Both B and C.

(13) Which organizational structure does this passage follow?

(A) Sequence

(B) Problem/solution

(C) Cause and effect

(D) Descriptive

(14) Which structure does the fourth paragraph of this passage follow?

(A) Sequence

(B) Cause and effect

(C) Descriptive organization

(D) Problem/solution

(15) The fifth paragraph of the passage is...

(A) Persuasive

(B) Informative

(C) Descriptive

(D) All of the above

Passage 4: The importance of artificial intelligence in human life. (For questions 16 through 20)

The term *artificial intelligence* is gaining more popularity these days. That is because it is gradually becoming an important part of our personal lives as well. Formerly, it was used only by businesses. However, with time, this technology is becoming more accessible to average people.

Advancements in machine learning and artificial intelligence are the reason behind the growing popularity of these technologies. Machines are integrated with IoT devices and robotics to think smart and work more efficiently. The advent of technology has provided these machines with human-like smartness and cognitive abilities.

These evolving machines adapt to their environment and perform much faster than their human counterparts. These machines can be programmed to do a specific task more precisely and effectively, even in the absence of their owners. This advancement has made artificial intelligent machines one of the most crucial parts of our day-to-day life.

Artificial intelligence technology and its components are no longer a new concept. They have been around for over a decade now. Artificially intelligent machines serve as tools that make this planet a better place to live. Previously, this technology could be seen only in fancy tech gadgets. However, that is no longer the case. Today, you will find various complex tasks that have been made easy through the integration of artificial intelligence.

This technology has made our lives easier. With time, it has turned into one of the biggest assets humans have. By programming these machines to take care of some of the most tedious day-to-day tasks, people gain time to focus on more important aspects of their lives. Designed to reduce human effort, these machines have the power to perform in an automated manner. They require minimal manual interaction.

This technology does much more than make the world error-free by simplifying complex tasks. It also finds its application in our everyday life and general activities. If you want to excel in this world, you should make this technology a part of your business and day-to-day life.

(16) What is the author's intent for this passage?

(A) To persuade

(B) To inform

(C) To educate

(D) Both B and C

(17) What is the main idea behind the second paragraph of this passage?

(A) Advancements in technology are the reason behind the popularity of AI-integrated machines.

(B) AI technology can only be used by businesses.

(C) Machine learning is an outdated technology.

(D) AI can change the world.

(18) Identify the topic sentence of the fourth paragraph.

(A) Artificial intelligence technology and its components are no longer a new concept.

(B) Artificially intelligent machines serve as tools that make this planet a better place to live.

(C) Previously, this technology could be seen only in fancy tech gadgets.

(D) Today, you will find various complex tasks that have been made easier through the integration of artificial intelligence.

(19) What is the author trying to discuss in the fifth paragraph?

(A) The benefits of artificial intelligence

(B) How artificial intelligence has changed human life

(C) How artificial intelligence has freed people from tedious tasks

(D) All of the above

(20) What is the author's intent behind the last paragraph?

(A) To persuade

(B) To inform

(C) To educate

(D) None of the above

Passage 5: The significance of living a minimal life. (For questions 21 through 25)

A minimal lifestyle is all about living your best life with less. There are various benefits of living frugally, including less debt, minimal expenses and fewer financial burdens. However, is it that easy to let go of your stuff?

The word *minimalism* carries a lot of weight these days. It has become a trend, and everyone is trying to jump on the bandwagon. Popular influencers are promoting minimalism. It has turned into more of an aesthetic rather than a way to minimize your expenses. Whether you do it for the Gram or to minimize the clutter, you get to save money in the end.

Minimalism has become a topic for the most popular podcasts. Documentaries have also been made, and there is a rise in the demand for books that teach minimalism. The intent is to show how living minimally can change your life for the better. It not only makes it easy to manage debt but helps you achieve a clean living space. This results in contentment and utmost peace of mind.

Those who truly understand minimalism know the philosophy behind this lifestyle. Minimalism is much more than getting rid of extra stuff you own. It is about acquiring the peace that comes with letting go of your worldly possessions. The philosophy of minimalism is based upon experiences rather than a materialistic mindset. Apart from freeing up your life financially, minimalism also offers mental emancipation that comes with owning less stuff.

If you consider minimalism a millennial fad, it is time to change your perspective. By practicing minimalism for the right reasons, you can rest assured that your life will change for the better. You will achieve financial stability in less time. Moreover, you will have less clutter to clean up every day.

(21) Which sentence did the author write to hook the readers?

(A) A minimal lifestyle is all about living your best life with less.

(B) There are various benefits of living frugally, including less debt, minimal expenses and fewer financial burdens.

(C) However, is it that easy to let go of your stuff?

(D) All of the above.

(22) Which of the following is the topic sentence in the second paragraph?

(A) The word *minimalism* carries a lot of weight these days.

(B) In fact, it has become a trend, and everyone is trying to jump on the bandwagon.

(C) Whether you do it for the Gram or to minimize clutter, you get to save money in the end.

(D) None of the above.

(23) What is the author trying to say in the third paragraph?

(A) Minimalism is the need of the hour.

(B) Documentaries and books about minimalism are more in demand these days.

(C) Minimalism saves you money.

(D) All of the above.

(24) Identify the topic sentence in the second-to-last paragraph.

(A) Those who truly understand minimalism know the philosophy behind this lifestyle.

(B) Minimalism is much more than getting rid of extra stuff you own.

(C) It is about acquiring the peace that comes with letting go of your worldly possessions.

(D) All of the above.

(25) The last paragraph of this passage is...

(A) Persuasive

(B) Informative

(C) Descriptive

(D) Narrative

Passage 6: How journaling disciplines your life. (For questions 26 through 30)

Journaling every day can change your life. It is one of the most powerful habits to acquire for those who want to bring more discipline to their lives. By journaling the right way, you can excel in every area of your life, be it personal or professional. According to those who journal every day, this activity helps a person make informed choices. People realize the worth of their time and therefore choose to use it wisely.

The habit of journaling is not an easy one to form. The reason most people give it up is that they fail even after trying several times. No matter how committed they are, they forget to journal when something comes up or they get busy. That said, journaling is an ideal way to declutter your mind when you have so much to do but do not know where to start. Penning your thoughts or doing a brain dump gives you a clear direction to pursue your goals for the day.

If you realize the benefits of journaling every day, you will not spend another day without journaling. You can optimize your creative potential with this activity. Working in the corporate market, you work on other people's terms. Every aspect of your life becomes aligned with the goals you have to achieve for others. As a result, you stop living intentionally. You feel like a machine that has been programmed to perform special functions, and you relive the same day over and over again.

If you want to restore control over your life, you need to start living intentionally. Journaling keeps you in touch with yourself and your personal goals, and it makes you more mindful. You feel more human and less machine-like. Journaling can be your creative outlet if you want it to be.

(26) What is the author's intent behind writing this piece?

(A) To inform

(B) To educate

(C) To persuade

(D) To describe

(27) What is the theme of this passage?

(A) The writer wants to educate readers about how journaling can change their lives.

(B) The writer believes journaling is a waste of time.

(C) According to the writer, journaling saves you time.

(D) The writer believes journaling is for kids.

(28) Identify the topic sentence in the second paragraph.

(A) The habit of journaling is not an easy one to form.

(B) The reason most people give it up is they fail even after trying several times.

(C) No matter how committed they are, they forget to journal when something comes up, or they get busy.

(D) None of the above.

(29) The third paragraph is...

(A) Persuasive

(B) Descriptive

(C) Informative

(D) Narrative

(30) Identify the author's point of view in this passage.

(A) First person

(B) Second person

(C) Third person

(D) Third-person limited omniscient

Test 1: Math Questions

(1) The teacher conducted a science test in a class of 10 students. The total score possible on the test was 30, and every student managed to score something. The students' test scores are listed in the table below. What is the mode?

20	21	25	21	15	30	21	17	04	21

(A) 21

(B) 24

(C) 20

(D) 40

(2) Robert solved the following equation and obtained the answer 26,500. However, the answer he calculated is wrong. What is the correct answer when the equation is x = 50 + 3 x (1000 ÷ 2)?

(A) 1,200

(B) 1,550

(C) 2,600

(D) 546

(3) Georgina wants to have a triangular mirror in her room. She also wants to decorate the borders of the mirrors with beautiful fairy lights. What is the length in meters of the fairy lights Georgina needs to cover her mirror's borders, provided that her triangular mirror is equilateral and one of its sides is 70 centimeters long?

(A) 210 meters

(B) 210 centimeters

(C) 2.1 meters

(D) 3,430 meters

(4) Sarah wants to measure the weight of an apple. She first needs to find the mass of the apple. What is the SI unit to measure the mass of an object?

(A) Liter

(B) Gram

(C) Milligram

(D) Kilogram

(5) If 1 hour has 60 minutes and 1 day contains 24 hours, how many minutes are there in 6 years?

(A) 52,560

(B) 3,153,600

(C) 360

(D) 131,400

(6) Emily's father has been diagnosed with kidney disease. The doctor has strictly advised the family to give the patient only five liters of water every day. Emily wants to make sure that her father drinks exactly five liters of water every day. Which of the following instruments should Emily use to measure the volume of water her father drinks daily?

(A) Measuring cylinder

(B) Meter ruler

(C) Inch tape measure

(D) Scale

(7) A boy has 20 chocolates that he needs to distribute among 40 kids. The boy finds out that for every two kids, he needs to keep one chocolate. Which of the following fractions is also a representation of the same information?

(A) 1/4

(B) 3/9

(C) 13/26

(D) 14/42

(8) Seven people are attending a party. The host orders a pizza that is divided into eight pieces. She wants to divide these eight pieces equally among all of the guests. Which of the following fractions best describes the portion of pizza each of the guests will get to eat?

(A) 1/8

(B) 7/8

(C) 8/7

(D) 1/2

(9) George took five tests in his annual examinations, and each test he took was worth 50 possible points. The table below represents George's annual report card and the scores he obtained. Calculate the total percentage he attained in his final exams.

Subject	Scores Obtained	Total Scores
Mathematics	41	50
English	45	50
Physics	34	50
Chemistry	46	50
Biology	31	50

(A) 50%

(B) 76%

(C) 64.6%

(D) 78.8%

(10) Ten people in a community recently joined the nearby gym. Their ages are 42, 64, 72, 23, 41, 35, 32, 10, 58 and x years. The gym manager needs to keep a track record of the attendees. Therefore, he determines the mean age of the 10 people, which is 39.1 years. Calculate the value of x. Also, find the median of their ages.

(A) x = 14 years; median = 38 years

(B) x = 10 years; median = 35 years

(C) x = 39 years; median = 41 years

(D) x = 54 years; median = 76 years

(11) Find two fractions with their denominators equal to 4 when the sum of the two fractions is equivalent to 3, and the difference between the two fractions is equal to 5.

(A) 16/4 and -4/4

(B) 12/4 and 1/4

(C) 4/16 and -2/4

(D) 3/4 and 5/4

(12) Simon scored 37.5% on his English test. Which of the following fractions best represents his test percentage?

(A) 9/64

(B) 3/8

(C) 37/100

(D) 37.5/50

(13) There are four types of books available in a school library that caters to 5,000 students. The books include course books, novels, biographies and magazines. Twenty-five percent of the students are interested in reading novels, 10% like to read course books, 60% are interested in reading biographies and the remaining students are fond of reading magazines. Which of the following types of graphs can best represent this data?

(A) Bar graph

(B) Line graph

(C) Pie chart

(D) Picture graph

(14) Clara wants to install a circular pond, 4 km in diameter, in her yard. She also wishes to surround it with a beautiful fence. How many meters of fence will she need to surround the pond?

(A) 13 meters

(B) 12,566 meters

(C) 1,300 meters

(D) 45,600 meters

(15) If $3^x \times 9 = 531{,}441$, what is the value of x?

(A) 02

(B) 12

(C) 10

(D) 14

(16) Sasha was playing golf with her friend Tina. Sasha managed to hit 34 balls into the holes, and Tina managed to hit 45 balls into the holes. Each of them was given 100 strokes to play. How many strokes did both of them miss in total?

(A) 121

(B) 21

(C) 100

(D) 50

(17) Andrew owns a large farm of 2,000 healthy cows. The mass of each cow is 2,500 kilograms. He sells 240 cows to one of his uncles and 635 cows to one of his fellow farmers. What is the total mass of cows in kilograms that Andrew is left with after making these two deals?

(A) 2,187

(B) 5,000

(C) 2,812.5

(D) 2,812,500

(18) There are 11 players on a cricket team. During a match between England and Australia, all 11 Australian cricketers get a chance to bat. The runs they score against England are 35, 100, 1, 54, 65, 76, 12, 20, 2, 15 and 37. What is the mean, median and mode of their runs?

(A) Mean: 37.9; Mode: None; Median: 35

(B) Mean: 32; Mode: 12; Median: 76

(C) Mean: 76; Mode: 0; Median 15

(D) Mean: 20; Mode: 0; Median 20

(19) What is the value of x when $16^x \div 64 = 4$?

(A) 3

(B) 2

(C) 16

(D) 0

(20) The area of a rectangular block is 50 cm². The length of that rectangular block is 5 m. What is the width of the rectangle in centimeters?

(A) 100 centimeters

(B) 1 centimeter

(C) 0.1 centimeter

(D) 10 centimeters

(21) Five hundred students took an exam. Twenty-four percent passed with flying colors, whereas 65% just barely passed. The remaining students failed. How many students out of 500 could not pass the examination?

(A) 55

(B) 50

(C) 24

(D) 11

(22) In a classroom, 56% of the students are girls. If the total number of students is 350, how many boys are there in the classroom?

(A) 196

(B) 56

(C) 154

(D) 44

(23) What is the value of z when z = 12 x (5² x 4) ÷ 6 + 11 − 6?

(A) 205

(B) 255

(C) 109

(D) 455

(24) Which of the following variables is mostly plotted on the x-axis of a graph?

(A) Control variable

(B) Dependent variable

(C) Independent variable

(D) None of the above

(25) Sarah and John went to watch a movie. The duration of the film was 2 hours 14 minutes. The movie started at 5:20 p.m. At what time did the film end?

(A) 7:34 p.m.

(B) 7:00 p.m.

(C) 7:34 a.m.

(D) 2:14 p.m.

(26) The base of a triangle is 5 cm less than three times the height of the triangle. If the triangle area is 100 cm², what are the height and the base of the triangle in meters?

(A) -7.4 meters and 5.4 meters

(B) -0.07 meters and 0.07 meters

(C) 0.09 meters and 0.22 meters

(D) 9 meters and 12 meters

(27) If a right-angled triangle is also an isosceles triangle, what will be the value of each of the two interior angles other than the right angle?

(A) 45 degrees

(B) 30 degrees

(C) 90 degrees

(D) 60 degrees

(28) A student wants to measure the time it takes to travel a certain distance by car. Which instrument should he use?

(A) A wall clock

(B) A stopwatch

(C) An hourglass

(D) Analog watch

(29) Which of the following exponents represents 5 x 5 x 5 x 5 x 5 x 5 x 5 x 5 the best?

(A) 10^8

(B) 5^8

(C) 10^4

(D) 5^7

(30) What is the value of y when $y = 3{,}566{,}703{,}139^0$?

(A) 3,566,703,139

(B) Zero

(C) One

(D) 3.556

Test 1: Writing Questions

For questions 1 through 6: In the sentences below, four words are underlined and have letters underneath. Read each sentence and select the underlined portion that contains a grammatical, word use, spelling or punctuation error. **None of the sentences has more than one error.**

(1) Tectonic plate theory <u>states</u> that the <u>Earth's</u> lithosphere is made of <u>plaits</u> of solid
                       A   B   C
crust that <u>move</u> and slide over the liquid mantle.
         D

(2) The <u>Mississippi</u> River is the second-longest river on the North American <u>continent</u>
        A   B
with a length of 2,348 miles and a <u>drainage</u> basin that <u>spanned</u> over 1.2 million miles.
                                         C   D

(3) The intertropical <u>convergence</u> zone or <u>equatorial</u> trough<u>,</u> is a zone a few hundred kilometers
                             A   B   C
wide in which winds blow inward and rise<u>,</u> releasing vast quantities of heat that
                                           D
stimulates convection.

(4) The purple-flowered <u>empress</u> tree, called the Paulownia tomentosa or foxglove tree,
                               A
<u>are</u> an invasive species of <u>deciduous</u> tree that can grow up to 20 feet tall in its first year
 B   C
and can achieve <u>maturity</u> in 10 years.
                D

(5) During the <u>last 30 years</u> of the nineteenth century, the United States <u>experienced</u>
               A   B
enormous industrial growth that <u>were</u> made possible by the expansion of the railways
                               C
<u>and</u> a rich supply of raw materials.
 D

(6) The <u>channelization</u> of the Kissimmee River in central Florida that <u>occurs</u> between
           A   B

1962 to 1971 had several impacts: from 2,000 to 14,000 hectares of wetlands were lost,
                                          C

groundwater started to become saline, <u>eutrophication</u> occurred in Lake Okeechobee,
                                                                    D

and there was widespread loss of animal and fish species.

(7) Alastair Burton has been given the assignment to write a short essay about the life of famous American writer Shelby Foote. He is searching for information. What kind of resource material should he use?

(A) Shelby Foote's written work

(B) An interview with Mr. Foote

(C) An article about Shelby Foote

(D) An encyclopedia

For questions 8 and 9: The following paragraph was written by a student named Genevieve for an assignment.

(1) It is said that compassion is priceless, but is it true? (2) When insulted, we humans fall off our path in righteous anger like men thwarted and belittled those who did them injury. (3) We harm and injure those who distress us. (4) We close those who try to help us. (5) We disregard the pain we cause, deeming it lesser than ours. (6) We seek not to understand but to vilify the evils of those who hurt us. (7) "Compassion is weak," we say. (8) Understanding grants nothing but misery. (9) Compassion is a gift that is to be given freely, without interest, without gaining anything in return. (10) Sometimes, it makes a world of difference.

(8) One of Genevieve's peers reviewed the essay and found himself confused by the word *close* used in sentence 4. Which of the following would be a good substitute for *close*?

(A) Turn our backs on

(B) Abandon

(C) Desert

(D) Forsake

(9) Upon further reflection, Genevieve realizes that *harm* and *injure* have a similar meaning. She decides to edit the sentence. Which of the following sentences would fit best into the paragraph without disrupting the syntactical structure?

(A) "I look down our nose at those who distressed me."

(B) "We condemn and ridicule those who scorn us."

(C) "We praise and magnify our achievements."

(D) "We malign and pull apart the strategy of those who hurt us."

(10) A <u>mudslide</u> can travel as fast as 35 miles per hour and can destroy everything in its path.

In the sentence above, the underlined word is being used as a:

(A) Noun

(B) Verb

(C) Subject

(D) Predicate

(11) Which of the following sentences contains word usage mistakes?

(A) The journalist wrote an article that was published in the *Times*.

(B) The tournament paired two teams of athletes verses two teams of hunter-gatherers.

(C) The woman leaped over the stream and landed on the other side.

(D) Uncle John and I went for a fishing trip to the Kissimmee River.

(12) Which of the following sentences is written in the passive voice?

(A) Alyssa sat on the couch and sighed.

(B) The book was read by Linda.

(C) Atlanta jogged across the street every morning.

(D) Brian looked at the sky and sighed.

(13) The following paragraph was written by a student.

I yawns and sat up from my bed. I tilted my head to the side. Surprisingly, no noises were filtering in from outside my room. I brushes my teeth, put on new clothes and opened my door. Silence greeted me. I could hear none of the dogs growling, nor any of the human chatter that usually made the house seem lively. A shiver of unease crawled up my spine. I feel shocked, uneasy and disquieted.

What is the primary error in this passage?

(A) Incorrect capitalization

(B) Run-on sentences

(C) Verb-tense errors

(D) Subject-verb disagreement

(14) Kiana has written a science-fiction fantasy novella for a competition. Currently, she is rearranging words and sentences, taking out and adding new parts to her story and replacing overused and unclear words. She is checking her writing for smoothness, clarity and pacing.

What stage of the writing process is she currently at?

(A) Proofreading

(B) Revising

(C) Drafting

(D) Researching

(15) Which punctuation mark is missing in the sentence below?

The building was built in 1763 it was constructed out of red brick and graced with marble floors and 20-foot-tall ceilings.

(A) Colon

(B) Comma

(C) Period

(D) Semicolon

(16) Which of the following words is not spelled correctly?

(A) Circuitious

(B) Tumult

(C) Camaraderie

(D) Amalgamation

(17) The continental crust is <u>over</u> 1,500 million years old on average, 35 to 70 km thick, has a lower density than oceanic crust and is composed of numerous types of rock.

In the sentence above, the underlined word is usually used as:

(A) A preposition

(B) A verb

(C) A subject

(D) An object

(18) Which sentence does not use correct capitalization?

(A) "It *Ends with Us* is a brilliant book," said the BookishBlogger in her review.

(B) Kieran studied engineering at the University of Nebraska.

(C) Alyssa and her aunt Anna completed their masters at the university of london in the United Kingdom.

(D) Hogan learned woodworking in Sweden.

(19) If the earth warms up more than 2° C over the next decade, small glaciers will disappear; huge swaths of coral will be destroyed; storms, forest fires, droughts and floods will increase in intensity; water will become scarce and crop yields will fall.

What is the simple predicate in the sentence above?

(A) more

(B) disappear

(C) warms

(D) destroyed

(20) About 252 million years ago, Earth's flora and fauna faced the largest extinction event in its history, the Permian-Triassic extinction event; this event nearly destroyed <u>all</u> life on Earth.

How is the underlined word being used in the sentence above?

(A) Verb

(B) Adverb

(C) Quantifier

(D) Interjection

(21) As a young <u>man</u> of twenty-four, his <u>mannerisms</u> were largely at <u>odds</u> with the rest of the society: they were larger <u>then</u> life.

Which word in the sentence above shows a grammatical construction, capitalization or punctuation error?

(A) odds

(B) mannerisms

(C) then

(D) man

(22) Which word is not spelled correctly?

(A) Wracked

(B) Tremors

(C) Hoarse

(D) Putrecence

(23) Criselda has been given the assignment to write a brief essay outlining the causes of the American Civil War. What kind of resource material would she find appropriate for her research?

(A) An encyclopedia

(B) Original written works like diaries, original research, interviews

(C) Books or articles that interpret original research

(D) Indexes

(24) Jeanne is checking her manuscript for any punctuation, word usage, grammatical construction, or capitalization errors that may have escaped her notice. Which stage of the writing process is Jeanne currently at?

(A) Revising

(B) Prewriting

(C) Drafting

(D) Editing

(25) In oceanic convection, cold salty water from polar regions, sinks into the depths of the ocean, and travels to the equator.

What is the punctuation error in the sentence above?

(A) Incorrect verb-tense use

(B) Sentence fragment

(C) Predicate disagreement

(D) Misplaced commas

(26) In 1912, Alfred Wegener <u>proposed</u> the theory of continental drift and suggested that about 250 million years ago, a huge single continent—which he named Pangea—broke apart and began to drift, eventually resulting in the continents we know today.

Which part of speech is underlined in the sentence above?

(A) Noun

(B) Verb

(C) Adjective

(D) Adverb

(27) In 2006, the Stern Review, a report by Sir Nicholas Stern, analyzed the financial implications of climate change and found that climate change is altering the planet, the risks of inaction are very high, and the time to make a difference has nearly run out.

What is the subject of the sentence written above?

(A) Sir Nicholas Stern

(B) Report

(C) The Stern Review

(D) 2006

For questions 28 and 29: These questions are based upon the rough draft of the starting paragraph of an essay written by a student named Alex Mohair.

Greenhouse Gases and Their Effect on Global Warming

(1) Greenhouse gases are essential for life on Earth. (2) Such as carbon dioxide, methane and carbon monoxide. (3) These gases allow shortwave radiation to pass through the atmosphere but trap outgoing long-wave radiation. (4) This heat warms the lower atmosphere of the earth, allowing life to flourish. (5) Global warming is caused because of the increasing concentration of greenhouse gases in the Earth's atmosphere. (6) Burning fossil fuels releases noxious gases that trap too much heat. (7) This excess heat increases the average temperature of the Earth and causes climate change. (8) Rivers dry up, deserts expand, and droughts and floods wreak havoc on the world's population.

(28) As Alex was proofreading his work, he realized that if he combined the first two sentences, the sentence that would be formed would be clear, concise and grammatically correct.

Which of the following combination of sentences 1 and 2 would be most effective?

(A) Greenhouse gases are essential for life on Earth, such as carbon dioxide, methane and carbon monoxide.

(B) Carbon dioxide, methane and carbon monoxide are greenhouse gases that are essential for life on Earth.

(C) To produce life on Earth, greenhouse gases, such as carbon dioxide, methane and carbon monoxide, are essential.

(D) Greenhouse gases, such as carbon dioxide, methane and carbon monoxide, are essential for life on Earth.

(29) One of Alex's teachers reviewed his essay and suggested to Alex that he should add a subordinating conjunction or transition word at the start of sentence 8 to clarify the relationship between cause and effect.

Which of the following subordinating conjunction would be most appropriate to place before the word *Rivers* in sentence 8?

(A) Furthermore

(B) As a result

(C) All in all

(D) Although

(30) Fossil records show that <u>eventually</u>, everything goes extinct; they show that over 99% of species that ever lived are extinct now.

How is the underlined word being used in the sentence above?

(A) As a noun

(B) As an adjective

(C) As an adverb

(D) As a verb

Essay Question: Some successful writers, such as Stephen King, claim that outlines are the last resource of bad fiction writers. In contrast, another extremely successful writer, John Grisham, claims that outlining is key to writing a good book.

Do you think writing an outline before starting your first draft is superior to writing without a plan? What are the advantages or disadvantages of writing an outline before your first draft? Write an essay explaining your argument.

Test 1: Reading Answers & Explanations

(1) (A) It explains what poaching is and how it impacts wildlife.

The main idea of this passage is to provide information on poaching. It informs readers how wildlife hunting turned from being a source of food for impoverished peasants to a popular sport for nobles and royalty. It also explains how poaching has negatively impacted wildlife.

(2) (C) At the beginning of the twentieth century, European feudal landowners claimed their right to hunt on the properties they owned.

This topic sentence provides the main idea for the paragraph. The main idea of this paragraph is how poaching turned into a crime.

(3) (D) Both B and C.

Supporting sentences support the main idea presented in the topic sentence. The main idea of this paragraph is how laws were imposed to keep peasants from hunting. Answers B and C support the facts presented in this paragraph.

(4) (A) A fact.

"These laws made subsistence poaching a more specialized activity in the eighteenth and nineteenth centuries." This sentence is a provable fact. It provides readers evidence in the form of dates.

(5) (C) To persuade.

This sentence suggests the writer intends to persuade the government to take action against animal poachers.

(6) (A) Environmental pollution and degradation are some of the biggest issues mankind is facing at present.

In the first paragraph, the writer introduces the main idea of the passage. The topic sentence of this paragraph informs readers that the passage will be discussing environmental pollution and degradation.

(7) (A) Human activity is causing the depletion of natural resources.

In the second paragraph, the author discusses how human activity is causing natural resources to be depleted. Option A successfully presents this idea.

(8) (A) A fact.

"According to the USDA (United States Development Authority) and the OECD (Organization for Economic Cooperation and Development), the increase in emission of greenhouse gases is negatively impacting earth." This sentence is a fact. The author supports the argument by adding solid references that a reader could research for veracity if so inclined.

(9) (C) To educate.

The author's intent is to educate readers about the consequences of increased human activity. The author's argument is supported with facts, statistics and reputable sources.

(10) (C) Third person.

This document is written in third person. That person is a detached observer, describing actions and impacts from afar. The narrator is not directly involved in the process.

(11) (B) In the last sentence.

The author introduces the main idea of the paragraph in the last sentence. In the first few lines, the author explains how the rise in eCommerce businesses has caused the increase in couponing. The last sentence explicitly states, "One of the best techniques to boost sales is to launch discount coupons," which lays the foundation for what the passage will be about.

(12) (D) Both B and C.

Facts are provable points that a reader can verify with research. In the passage, both B and C state a fact. "The first coupon was launched by Coca-Cola in1887." In this sentence, the author mentions the year when the first coupon was launched. This date can easily be confirmed with some quick research, which makes it a fact. Similarly, research can quickly confirm that "Businesses have been engaging customers through marketing campaigns for over a hundred years."

(13) (D) Descriptive.

The structure of this passage is descriptive. The author informs readers about the importance of couponing and how it benefits both the business and its customers. It also explains what is causing an increase in the use of coupons. In the final paragraph, the author persuades the readers to try couponing. However, the majority of the passage is descriptive.

(14) (B) Cause and effect.

In the fourth paragraph, the author explains what is causing more consumers to use coupons to save money. That textual structure is cause and effect.

(15) (A) Persuasive.

The fifth paragraph is persuasive. The author persuades readers to collect and redeem coupons just like their favorite celebrities do.

(16) (B) To inform.

The author in this passage intends to inform readers about artificial intelligence and the endless possibilities it offers. The passage informs readers of how technology has changed our lives for good and how it should be incorporated into each area of our lives.

(17) (A) Advancements in technology are the reason behind the popularity of AI-integrated machines.

This paragraph's main idea is how technological advancements have increased the demand for AI-based machines.

(18) (B) Artificially intelligent machines serve as tools that make this planet a better place to live.

In this paragraph, the second sentence is the topic sentence. It tells you what the rest of the passage will be about.

(19) (D) All of the above.

In the fifth paragraph, the writer lists the benefits of artificial intelligence technology. The author discusses how this groundbreaking technology has made our lives easier. This paragraph explains how integrating this technology gives you more time to spend with your family without compromising your productivity.

(20) (A) To persuade.

In the last paragraph, the author intends to persuade readers to integrate AI into their lives if they want to excel. The author discusses AI's benefits and then switches to a persuasive tone, which emphasizes the significance of AI in personal and professional life.

(21) (C) However, is it that easy to let go of your stuff?

An author often uses a question at the start or the end of an introductory paragraph to hook readers. The first paragraph of this passage ends with a question to entice the reader into reading the rest of the passage.

(22) (A) The word *minimalism* carries a lot of weight these days.

In the second paragraph, the topic sentence is "The word *minimalism* carries a lot of weight these days," which is what the whole paragraph is about.

(23) (D) All of the above.

In the third paragraph, the writer tries to explain how minimalism's positive effects have become a common topic of conversation these days, from documentaries to books.

(24) (B) Minimalism is much more than getting rid of extra stuff you own.

In the second-to-last paragraph, the topic sentence introduces the philosophy behind the concept of minimalism.

(25) (A) Persuasive.

The last paragraph of this passage is persuasive. The author is trying to convince readers to adopt minimalistic practices to achieve both financial stability and peace of mind.

(26) (C) To persuade.

The author's intent behind writing this text is to persuade readers to take up journaling as a hobby. The author lists the benefits of journaling in the first few paragraphs and suggests readers adopt the habit of journaling to add more discipline to their life.

(27) (A) The writer wants to educate readers about how journaling can change their lives.

In this passage, the writer wants to show the reader how journaling is a great habit. The author lists the benefits of journaling in order to persuade readers to take it up as a hobby. Therefore, the theme of the passage is the benefits of journaling.

(28) (A) The habit of journaling is not an easy one to form.

This topic sentence indicates that readers need to put forth effort in order to adopt journaling as a habit, which is what the paragraph is about.

(29) (C) Informative.

The third paragraph is informative. The writer informs readers about the benefits of journaling.

(30) (C) Third person.

In this passage, the author uses third person, acting as a detached observer who is sharing a universal experience with the audience.

Test 1: Math Answers & Explanations

(1) (A) 21.

Mode is the most repeated value in the data. In this data, 21 is repeated four times and more than any other grade. This is why it is the mode.

(2) (B) 1,550.

Apply the PEMDAS rule: P (parentheses), E (exponents), M (multiplication), D (division), A (addition) and S (subtraction).

First, open the parentheses and divide 1,000 by 2 to obtain 500.

x = 50 + 3 x 500

Multiply 3 by 500 to obtain 1,500.

x = 50 + 1,500

Add 50 to 1,500 to obtain the final answer, 1,550.

Robert obtained the wrong answer because he followed the wrong pattern;

He first added 3 to 50.

x = 53 (1,000 ÷ 2)

He then divided 1,000 by 2 to obtain 500.

x = 53 (500)

Lastly, he multiplied 53 with 500 to obtain 26,500, which is the wrong answer. He did not follow PEMDAS.

(3) (C) 2.1 meters.

An equilateral triangle has three sides that are equal in length. Therefore, if one of the sides is 70 centimeters long, then all three sides of this triangle are 70 cm long. To find the required length of the fairy lights, Georgina needs to find the perimeter of the triangle. The perimeter of the triangle is the sum of the lengths of the three sides.

Add 70 three times to obtain 210.

70 + 70 + 70 = 210 centimeters

1 centimeter is equal to 1/100 meters

Hence, 210 centimeters are equal to 210/100, which equals 2.1 meters.

(4) (D) Kilogram.

SI units are the standard units of measurements set by the International System of Units for the seven base quantities, including the mass of an object. The SI base unit for the mass is the kilogram.

(5) (B) 3,153,600.

One year contains 365 days. One day contains 24 hours, and 1 hour consists of 60 minutes. Therefore, in 6 years, there are 6 x 365 x 24 x 60 minutes, which is equal to 3,153,600.

(6) (A) Measuring cylinder.

A meter ruler and inch tape measure are used to measure lengths. A scale is used to measure the mass of an object. However, to measure the volume of liquid, a measuring cylinder is used.

(7) (C) 13/26.

Taking each option:

For 3/9; both 3 and 9 are divisible by 3.

3 divided by 3 is equal to 1, and 9 divided by 3 is equal to 3. The most simplified form of 3/9 is 1/3.

For 14/42, both 14 and 42 are divisible by 14.

14 divided by 14 is equal to 1, and 42 divided by 14 is equal to 3. The most simplified form of 14/42 is 1/3.

However, for 13/26, both are divisible by 13.

13 divided by 13 is equal to 1, and 26 divided by 13 is equal to 2. The final answer is 1/2.

(8) (C) 8/7.

When eight pieces of pizza are divided among seven people attending the party, the fraction will be 8/7. This is because 1/8 denotes the division of one piece among eight people, 7/8 signifies the division of seven pieces among eight people, and 1/2 denotes that for every two people, there is one piece of pizza.

(9) (D) 78.8%.

To calculate the percentage, the formula is:

(Obtained scores/total scores possible) x 100

In this case, obtained scores are 197, and the total scores possible are 5 x 50 = 250.

Hence, (197/250) x 100 is 78.8%.

(10) (A) x = 14 years; median = 38 years.

The mean is the average of the data. The formula to calculate the mean is:

Mean = sum of data/total number of data

The sum of data is 377 + x, and the total number of data is 10.

39.1 = 377 + x/10

Multiply 39.1 with 10 to obtain 391.

391 = 377 + x

Subtract 377 from 391 and obtain 14 as the value of x.

The median is the middle value. To find the median, you first need to arrange the terms in ascending order (from smallest to largest).

If the total number of data is an even number, such as 10 in this case, there are two middle values where the median lies between the n/2nd and (n + 2)/2nd position. Hence, the median lies between n/2 = 10/2 = the fifth place, and (n + 2)/2 = 12/2 = the sixth place in this data.

10, 14, 23, 32, 35, 41, 42, 58, 64, 72 is the new order of the data in the ascending order.

In the fifth place, the age is 35 years, and in the sixth place, the age is 41 years.

To find the median for this data, add these two middle values and divide the sum by 2.

35 + 41 = 76

76/2 = 38. The median age of the gym members is 38 years.

(11) (A) 16/4 and -4/4.

Let the numerator of one fraction be x and the numerator of the other fraction be y.

Create two equations.

x/4 + y/4 = 3 and x/4 − y/4 = 5

Take equation 1:

x/4 + y/4 = 3.

Multiply 4 with 3 to remove the denominator and obtain x + y = 12.

Make x the subject of the formula x = 12 − y.

Take equation 2:

x/4 − y/4 = 5

Multiply 4 with 5 to remove the denominator and obtain x − y = 20.

Substitute the value of x from equation 1 in equation 2.

12 − y − y = 20

Add the two ys, and subtract 12 from 20.

-2y = 8

Divide 8 by -2 and obtain the value of y, which is -4.

Substitute the value of y in the first equation to obtain the value of x.

x = 12 – (-4)

When two minus signs multiply, they add up. Hence, 12 + 4 will give 16 as the value of x.

Since the value of x is 16 and y is -4, the fractions with denominator 4 will become 16/4 and -4/4.

(12) (B) 3/8.

To remove the percentage sign, you first need to divide the percentage by 100.

37.5% = 37.5/100

This fraction is not the final answer because it can be further simplified and divided.

Both 37.5 and 100 are divisible by 12.5.

37.5 divided by 12.5 is equal to 3, and 100 divided by 12.5 is equal to 8.

No number can be divided by both 3 and 8.

Thus, the final and most simplified version of 37.5% or 37.5/100 is 3/8.

(13) (C) Pie chart.

A pie chart is the most suitable graphic representation when you intend to show the composition of something. Each slice of the pie can help you present a different category. Therefore, a pie chart is the best option for representing different types of books and the percentage of students interested in them.

(14) (B) 12,566 meters.

To find the length of the fence Clara needs to surround her circular pond, she first needs to find the perimeter/circumference of the pond.

The diameter of the pond is 4 km.

Radius is half of the diameter.

Therefore, radius of the pond = diameter/2 = 4/2 = 2 km.

The formula for the perimeter of a circle:

Circumference = $2\pi r$.

Substitute the value of radius in the formula.

Circumference = $2(\pi)(2)$ = 12.566 km

1 kilometer = 1 x 1,000 meters.

Therefore, 12.566 kilometers = 12.566 x 1,000 meters.

The final answer for the circumference of the circle in meters is 12,566 meters.

Clara needs 12,566 meters of fence to surround the circular pond in her house.

(15) (C) 10.

9 can be written as 3 x 3, which in turn can also be written as 3^2.

531,441 can be written as 3 x 3 x 3 x 3 x 3 x 3 x 3 x 3 x 3 x 3 x 3 x 3, and this in turn can also be written as 3^{12}.

Hence, $3^x \times 9 = 531,441$ can also be written as $3^x \times 3^2 = 3^{12}$.

Taking the left-hand side:

When the bases are the same and the terms are multiplied, their powers add up.

In this case, the base is 3 and is the same for both the terms.

Therefore, it can be written as $3^{x+2} = 3^{12}$.

Moreover, when the bases on both sides are the same with an = sign in between, their powers are also equal.

Therefore, the equation can also be written as x + 2 = 12.

Subtract 2 from 12.

x = 12 − 2

Obtain the final answer of x, which is 10.

(16) (A) 121.

Sasha got 100 strokes. She managed to hit 34 holes.

To find how many strokes she missed, subtract 34 from 100.

100 − 34 = 66. Sasha missed 66 strokes.

Tina also got 100 strokes. She managed to hit 45 holes.

To find how many strokes she missed, subtract 45 from 100.

100 − 45 = 55. Tina missed 55 strokes.

In total, both women were given 200 strokes.

To find how many holes both Tina and Sasha missed in total:

Add the holes missed by each of them. Sasha missed 66, and Tina missed 55.

66 + 55 = 121.

Tina and Sasha together missed 121 holes in total.

(17) (C) 2,812.5.

The mass of each cow is 2,500 kilograms.

Andrew has 2,000 healthy cows.

Andrew sold 240 cows to his uncle and 635 cows to his fellow farmer.

To find the total number of cows he sold, add the two.

240 + 635 = 875

Andrew sold 875 cows. To find the number of cows he has after selling 875 cows, subtract 875 from 2,000, which is the total number of cows he originally had.

2000 − 875 = 1125

After selling 875 cows, Andrew now has 1,125 cows.

To find the total mass of 1,125 cows, multiply 1,125 with 2,500 kilograms.

1,125 x 2,500 = 2,812,500.

The total mass of 1,125 cows in grams in 2,812,500 kilograms.

1 gram = 1/1000 kilograms.

To find the mass of the remaining cows in kilograms, divide 2812500 by 1000.

2812500/1000 is equal to 2812.5 kilograms.

(18) (A) Mean: 37.9; Mode: None; Median: 35.

35, 100, 1, 54, 65, 76, 12, 20, 2, 15 and 37 are the runs scored by the 11 cricketers of the Australian cricket team.

The formula for calculating mean is:

Mean = sum of data ÷ total number of data

The total number of data is 11.

Mean = (35 + 100 + 1 + 54 + 65 + 76 + 12 + 20 + 2 + 15 + 37) ÷ 11

Add the runs score by the players to obtain the sum of data.

Mean = 417/11

Divide 417 by 11 to obtain the final value of mean, which is equal to approximately 37.9.

For mode:

Mode is the most repeated value in the data. In this set of data, there is no value that is repeated. Therefore, there exists no mode in these runs scored by the 11 cricketers.

For median:

Median is the middle value of the data.

To find the median, you first need to arrange the data in ascending order.

1, 2, 12, 15, 20, 35, 37, 54, 65, 76, 100 is the new order of the data.

After arranging the data in ascending order, find the middle value of the data.

To find the position of the median when the total number of data is an odd number, the formula is (n + 1)/2, where n denotes the number of data.

The median for this data lies in the (11 + 1)/2 = 12/2 = sixth position.

In the sixth place, the value is 35. Hence, 35 is the median for the data.

So, the mean is 37.9; the mode is none and the median is 35.

(19) (B) 2.

16 can be written as 4 x 4, and 4 x 4 can be written as 4^2.

64 can be written as 4 x 4 x 4, and 4 x 4 x 4 can be written as 4^3.

If any number does not have a power, it means that the power of that number is 1.

Therefore, 4 can be written as 4^1.

Hence, $16^x \div 64 = 4$ can be written as $(4^2)^x \div 4^3 = 4^1$.

$(4^2)^x$ can also be written as 4^{2x} because the powers have multiplied with each other.

Taking the left-hand side:

When the bases of the terms are the same and the terms are being divided, the powers on the terms subtract.

Therefore, $4^{2x} \div 4^3$ can be written as 4^{2x-3}.

When the bases on both sides of the equations are the same with an = sign in between, the powers are also equal.

Therefore, $2x - 3 = 1$.

Add 3 to 1 to obtain 4.

2x = 4

Divide 4 by 2.

x = 4/2 = 2

The final value of x is 2.

(20) (C) 0.1 centimeters.

1 meter = 1 x 100 = 100 centimeters

Therefore, 5 meters = 5 x 100 = 100 centimeters.

The length of the rectangle is 500 centimeters.

The formula for the area of a rectangle:

Area = length x width

The area of the rectangle is 50 cm².

Width = area/length.

Substitute the value of area and length in the formula.

Width = 50/500

Divide 50 by 500.

The value for width is 0.1 centimeters.

(21) (A) 55.

First, calculate the number of students who passed the exam either with flying colors or just barely.

Out of 500 students, 24% passed with flying colors.

To remove the % sign, divide 24% by 100 and obtain 24/100.

To calculate the number of students who passed with flying colors, multiply 24/100 by 500.

(24/100) x 500 = 120 students

65% of 500 students just barely passed the examination.

To remove the % sign, divide 65 by 100 and obtain 65/100.

To calculate the number of students who just passed the examination, multiply 65/100 with 500.

(65/100) x 500 = 325 students

To calculate the total number of students who passed the exam either with flying colors or just barely, add the two.

325 + 120 = 445 students passed.

To calculate the number of students who failed, subtract 445 from 500.

500 − 445 = 55 students failed to pass the examination.

(22) (C) 154.

The total number of students in a class is 350.

Girls make up 56% of the students.

To remove the % sign, divide 56% by 100 and obtain 56/100.

To obtain the number of girls in the class, multiply 56/100 by 350.

(56/100) x 350 = 196 girls

To find the number of boys, subtract 196 from 350.

350 − 196 = 154 boys in the class.

(23) (A) 205.

Apply PEMDAS to solve 12 x (5^2 x 4) ÷ 6 + 11 − 6.

Open the parentheses by first solving the exponents.

$5^2 = 5 \times 5 = 25$,

Next, multiply.

$25 \times 4 = 100$.

Multiply again.

$12 \times (100) = 1200$

Next, divide.

$1200 \div 6 = 200$

Next, add.

$200 + 11 = 211$

Finally, subtract.

$z = 211 - 6 = 205$

(24) (C) Independent variable.

On the x-axis, which is the horizontal axis of the graph, we mostly plot the independent variable. On the y-axis of the graph, we mostly plot the dependent variable.

The independent variable is the variable that is not affected by any change in the experiment.

The dependent variable is the variable that is affected by the changes in control variables, independent variable or any other variable present in the experiment.

Control variables are kept constant in an experiment to increase the reliability of the results.

(25) (A) 7:34 p.m.

The film started at 5:20 p.m. In this representation of time, 5 denotes the hour and 20 denotes the minutes passed.

The duration of the film is 2 hours and 14 minutes. Add the hours 5 + 2 to obtain 7:20 p.m. Then, add the 14 minutes in the 20 minutes passed to obtain 34 minutes. Hence, when the film is over, the clock will show 7:34 p.m.

(26) (C) 0.09 meters and 0.22 meters.

Let the height of the triangle be x.

Three times the height of the triangle is 3x, and 5 less than three times the height is 3x − 5. Therefore, the base of the triangle is 3x − 5.

The formula for the area of a triangle is:

Area of triangle = 1/2 x base x height

The area of the triangle is 100 cm².

Substitute the expression of base, height and the value of area in the formula.

100 = 1/2 x (3x − 5) (x)

Multiply the 2 on the right-hand side with 100 on the left to obtain 200.

200 = x (3x − 5)

Multiply x with 3x and 5 to obtain 3x² and 5x.

200 = 3x² − 5x

Take 200 on the right-hand side to obtain a quadratic equation.

3x² − 5x − 200 = 0

To find two values of x, use the quadratic formula.

Quadratic formula is x = (-b ± √ (b² − 4ac))/ 2a, where a = 3, b = -5 and c = -200.

The two values of x are 9.04 and -7.37.

Since length is a scalar quantity and cannot be negative, -7.37 will be rejected.

The height x of the triangle is 9.04 centimeters.

1 centimeter is equal to 1/100 meters.

Therefore, 9 centimeters are equal to 9/100 meters, which is 0.09 meters.

Also, 5 centimeters are equal to 5/100 meters, which is 0.05 meters.

To find the base of the triangle in meters, substitute the value of x in its expression, 3x − 5.

$3(0.09) - 0.05 = 0.22$.

The base of the triangle is 0.22 meters.

(27) (A) 45 degrees.

For a triangle to be right-angled, one of the angles needs to be 90 degrees. On the other hand, if a triangle is isosceles, two of its sides and angles are equal. The sum of the interior angles of a triangle is 180 degrees.

Let one of the unknown angles be x. Since two of them are equal, let the unknown angles be 2x.

$2x + 90 = 180$.

Subtract 90 from 180 to obtain 90 degrees.

$2x = 90$

Divide 90 by 2.

$x = 90/2 = 45$ degrees

(28) (B) A stopwatch.

The stopwatch gives the most accurate time. You can start it when you start the experiment and stop it when you end the experiment. The hourglass is an ancient method of measuring time and is not precise. There is a chance of significant error in analog watches and a wall clock, such as parallax error and human reaction time.

(29) (B) 5^8.

Since 5 is written eight times in 5 x 5 x 5 x 5 x 5 x 5 x 5 x 5, it can be written as 5^8.

To verify, 5 x 5 x 5 x 5 x 5 x 5 x 5 x 5 is 390,625.

$10^8 = 100,000,000$

$10^4 = 10,000$

$5^7 = 78,125$

On the other hand, $5^8 = 390,625$. Therefore, the correct value is 5^8.

(30) (C) One.

If a number has zero as its power, it will always be equal to one, no matter how large or small the number may be.

Test 1: Writing Answers & Explanations

(1) (C) Plaits.

The word *plaits* means a *braid*. This word is a homophone. It sounds similar to the word *plate*—a flat dish—which is written differently and has a different meaning. This word is written incorrectly and is an example of a word usage error.

(2) (D) Spanned.

This is a verb-tense error. The whole sentence is written in the present tense, as indicated by the state-of-being verb *is*. In contrast, the verb *spanned* is written in past tense. So, out of all the options presented, Option D is correct, as it has an identifiable grammatical construction error.

(3) (C) ,

In this sentence, a comma is used to separate the subject from the verb. Commas cannot be used to separate a subject from a verb in an independent clause.

(4) (B) are.

The plural form of a stative verb is used in this sentence. In the sentence, the subject is one single empress tree as indicated by the singular noun *tree* at the start of the sentence. Since the subject is singular, the stative verb should also be singular (*is*) instead of plural (*are*). Out of all the options presented, Option B contains an identifiable subject-verb disagreement.

(5) (C) were.

The plural form of a stative verb is used in this sentence. In this case, the stative verb *were*—the plural form of *was*—is used after a singular subject. This creates a jarring rhythm and is grammatically incorrect because you cannot use a plural verb with a singular subject.

(6) (B) occurs.

The present form of a verb is used in this sentence. *Occurs* is a verb used in the present tense. A time in the past is mentioned in the sentence, "1962 to 1971," along with the verb *had*, which is used further in the sentence. This lends further credence to the fact that the verb *occurs* does not belong in its current form in the sentence.

(7) (C) An article about Shelby Foote.

Finding an article about Shelby Foote is a practical, efficient way of researching a short essay.

(8) (D) forsake.

The tone of the whole paragraph is a bit melodramatic, slightly philosophical and a bit enigmatic. All four options are synonyms for each other. Option A, *Turn our backs on,* is too colloquial and breaks the paragraph's mood. Option B, *abandon,* has similar problems. Option C, *desert,* could be used, but it does not carry the whole paragraph's tone very well. Thus, the word that best matches the paragraph's tone while adding clarity to the sentence can only be *forsake.*

(9) (B) "We condemn and ridicule those who scorn us."

The first option diverges too much from the original sentence's meaning and changes the point of view from third-person plural *we* to first-person singular *I.* Option C is the opposite of the original sentence, while Option D discusses an entirely new aspect that is not addressed in the original paragraph. This leaves Option B.

(10) (C) Subject.

The first option could be correct because *mudslide* is a noun. If this word was found anywhere else in the sentence, this option could be correct. However, Option C negates it. The subject shows what a sentence is about. *Mudslide* is the subject of the sentence because the whole sentence talks about it.

(11) (B) The tournament paired two teams of athletes verses two teams of hunter-gatherers.

The word *verses* in Option B is a homophone. It sounds the same as *versus*, but it has an entirely different meaning. A verse is a single metrical line. *Versus*, on the other hand, is a preposition that means "against or in contrast to."

(12) (B) The book was read by Linda.

A sentence is in the active voice when the subject performs an action, such as "Dana ran across the lawn." A sentence is passive when the subject is being acted upon by the verb. i.e., "The book was read by Linda."

(13) (C) Verb-tense errors.

There are no instances of incorrect capitalization, run-on sentences or subject-verb errors present in the paragraph. However, the paragraph has several verb-tense errors. In the first sentence, the verbs *yawns* and *sat* clash. *Yawns* is a present-tense verb, while *sat* is the past form of *sit*. Later, the verb *brushes* clashes with the verb *opened*.

(14) (B) Revising.

During revision, the first draft gets rearranged. Some sentences and words are added, and others are taken out. There is no major rearranging done at the editorial stage. In the research stage of the writing process, you search for information. During drafting, words are usually written rather than cut out. This leaves Option B as the only correct option.

(15) (D) Semicolon.

A semicolon is used between two independent clauses. In this sentence, both the clauses on the sides of the blank have a subject and a verb; thus, they can be classified as independent clauses. A colon is used to introduce something, such as a list. A period is used to complete a sentence, and a comma cannot be used between two independent clauses.

(16) (A) Circuitious.

Tumult, camaraderie and *amalgamation* are correct. *Circuitous* is written as *circuitious*. An extra *i* has been added before the *o*.

(17) (A) A preposition.

Over is usually classified as a preposition in English. In this sentence, *over* means "more than." It cannot be used as a verb, though it can be used as an adverb. It also cannot be used as the subject of any sentence. The word *over* cannot be the object of the sentence because it is not a noun or pronoun.

(18) (C) Alyssa and her aunt Anna completed their masters at the university of london in the United Kingdom.

Option A is properly capitalized. The book name and the blogger's name are proper nouns. Proper nouns are the specific names of people, things, places and ideas. All proper nouns present in Option B and D are also capitalized. But, in Option C, the university's name is a proper noun and should be capitalized.

(19) (C) warms.

In this case, the verb that tells what the subject does is *warms. Earth* is the subject of the sentence. The verb that comes immediately after is *warms*. This verb determines the action of the subject.

(20) (C) Quantifier.

A determiner is a word that introduces a noun. It is usually placed before a noun in a sentence. Determiners have to be used before a singular noun (*a dog*) and are usually not needed for a plural noun. The underlined word *all* is a determiner. It is used before the noun *life*. In this case, this particular determiner is called a quantifier. Quantifiers are determiners that tell how much or how little a noun is being used. So, Options A, B and D are incorrect.

(21) (C) then.

The word *then* is used to show an action that takes place in relation to time (to show what comes next or what used to be). For example, "Alya went to school, then she walked back home." The word *than* is used to make a comparison between two things. In this case, *than* should be used because a comparison is being made in the sentence. Using *then* instead of *than* is a word usage error.

(22) (D) Putrecence.

The first three options are correct. Option D, *putrecence,* has a missing *s* between *re* and *ce*. *Putrecence* should be written as *putrescence*.

(23) (C) Books or articles that interpret original research.

Since Criselda has to write a brief essay, she does not need to gather a great deal of information. She just needs the basic facts. She does not need to peruse original or primary documents because they are usually hard to get and such research is time-consuming. Indexes would be good if she has to search out primary resources or obscure secondary resources. An encyclopedia is useless because it would not contain more than the bare bones of the conflict. That leaves books and articles as the best resource material for Criselda's short essay.

(24) (D) Editing.

The phrase "escaped her notice" gives a clue to the stage of the writing process Jeanne is currently at. Prewriting is done before writing the manuscript. During revision, huge chunks of words are cut out, added and shifted throughout the manuscript for better pacing and clarity. Drafting happens when the writer begins writing the actual essay. Jeanne is past all that. This leaves editing. Editing is a part of the writing process when any residual errors in the text are weeded out with a fine-toothed comb.

(25) (D) Misplaced commas.

Sinks is separated from the rest of the sentence due to incorrect comma placement. The other comma is situated behind the coordinate conjunction *and,* where it is not needed.

(26) (B) Verb.

A verb (*proposed*) is underlined in the sentence. The part of speech can be identified as a verb because it shows the action in the sentence.

(27) (C) The Stern Review.

The Stern Review is the subject of the sentence written above because the whole sentence talks about what the Stern Review discovered. In the sentence, the Stern Review analyzes the financial consequences of climate change. It is the thing that is performing an action.

(28) (D) Greenhouse gases, such as carbon dioxide, methane and carbon monoxide, are essential for life on Earth.

Option A is an unimproved copy of the two sentences. It adds nothing to the essay. Option B turns the active sentence into a passive sentence. Option C changes the subject of the sentence and makes it unsuitable to be used as the first sentence for an essay focusing on greenhouse gases. Option D uses the examples as an essential adverbial clause between the sentences. This creates a good starting sentence that is also grammatically sound.

(29) (B) As a result.

Furthermore cannot be selected because it is a conjunction that is used to make an additional point in an argument. It is not used to show the consequence of something. *Although* cannot be used before the sentence because it means "in spite of" and is used to link two dissimilar ideas. *All in all* means that you have reached a conclusion after considering every aspect of the problem or situation. *As a result* is a conjunctive adverb phrase that is used to show cause-and-effect relationships.

(30) (C) As an adverb.

Adverbs are words that are used to describe a verb, another adverb, adjectives or any other types of phrases or words. Adverbs give more information about the subject of a sentence. In this sentence, the underlined word is an adverb.

Essay Question: Sample Response

The first time I tried to write a novel, I started without a plan. Armed with my zeal and enthusiasm, I started penning my work on individual sheaves of paper every day. As leaves dried and fell from trees, my pile of sheaves grew until I finally hit a wall. I did not know where to go from there. This kind of spontaneous writing is called pantsing or writing without an outline.

An outline is a plan that describes what a writer wants to include in his or her book. Outlines can be as detailed or as sparse as a writer desires. Outlining can work wonders for some writers, while for others, it can create unnecessary hurdles.

First of all, outlining can offer more control over the writing process. Big-name authors like Brandon Sanderson and John Grisham swear that outlining what will happen in a book before writing can have very nice results. Plot holes, pacing issues and timeline issues can easily be identified and corrected ahead of time. Intricate foreshadowing and plot devices can be employed during writing because the whole plot is already known to the writer. Subplots can be created. Plot slumps can be avoided. Character arcs can be woven with much more finesse. A good example of a series that had extensive outlining before the first book was written is the *Age of Madness* trilogy by Joe Abercrombie. Joe worked on the plot, characters and worldbuilding extensively before putting his pen to paper. This, according to him, helped him produce a better product.

Another benefit of outlining is that it gives a writer better control over plot lines. The best-selling *Mistborn* trilogy was published consecutively over three years by Brandon Sanderson in the 2000s. Sanderson had planned the major events, character arcs and plot lines for all three books before starting. The books were cohesive and intricate, with overarching conflicts, clever foreshadowing, fluid plotlines and multitudes of subplots. In contrast, later books in the *Mistborn* series were not as cohesive as their predecessors. This shows that outlining before writing can help build much more refined and plot-focused books. It can help a writer build tight plots and channel the story toward one direction rather than letting it meander everywhere or quitting halfway through.

On the other hand, outlining before writing can also become tedious and constraining. Some writers may abandon their work and never come back to it because of its stifling nature. Oftentimes, very intricate outlines can leave the writer with no room to move. Excessive outlining can also stifle creativity, so some authors like Robin Hobb—the best-selling author of the *Farseer* Series—and J.K. Rowling prefer a looser outline where they can make changes if they think the changes would improve or add something to the book.

Furthermore, sometimes intricate outlining can take the joy out of writing because the writer knows the character motivations, plot lines and character arcs ahead of time. So, there remains no excitement in finding out the rest while writing.

In conclusion, outlining can greatly enhance the quality of a written work by allowing the writer to make it more intricate and well put together. However, outlining can also smother the spark of creativity and stifle the excitement of writing a new story. The choice of writing an outline or not simply depends on an author's preferred personal writing style.

Test 2: Reading Questions

Carefully read the passages below and answer the question at the end of each passage.

Passage 1: The evolution of the fashion industry. (For questions 1 through 5)

Before the industrialization of the fashion industry, people used to wear dresses made from handspun fabric. These fabrics were made through the time-consuming process of hand warping. These dresses were worn, resized, reused and mended over and over again until they were beyond repair. Even their scraps were used to stuff pillows, cushions and sometimes furniture.

Homemade clothes were not limited to lower-class families. Even the rich had quite a few options when it came to fashion. If you are a reader of Edith Wharton's books, it is easier for you to imagine how limited the options were back in the nineteenth century. Each year, women from rich families made one trip to Paris to update their annual wardrobe. They always preferred quality over quantity.

However, things changed with the advent of the latest technologies in the field of fashion. These technologies were fairly simple in the beginning and included the spinning jenny, standard-sizing systems and sewing machines. These machines made it possible to design and wear ready-made clothing. These dresses were low cost, as they did not require much effort to be manufactured.

With the drop in prices of haute couture, the latest designs and stylish fabrics became more accessible to people at all levels of society. However, with lower prices, fabric became rather disposable. Even those within lower income brackets could afford more clothes than they previously did.

This provided mainstream clothes manufacturers with an opportunity to grow their business. They launched several collections every year. This caused the rise of the "fast fashion" industry we know today. This consumerist approach to fashion has made it difficult for everyone to keep up with the latest fashion trends.

The days when a piece of clothing could last you a lifetime are long gone. People invest in fast fashion to keep up with the latest trends. This is causing not only more pollution but also a rise in the prices of fast fashion items. The worst part is, despite being expensive, these fashions barely last a season.

(1) Identify the words that start with vowels in the first paragraph.

(A) Industrialization, industry, of, use

(B) Stuff, pillows, cushions, furniture

(C) Time-consuming, hand warping, handspun

(D) None of the above

(2) Identify the antonyms in the second paragraph.

(A) Lower-class/rich

(B) Quality/quantity

(C) Update/preferred

(D) All of the above

(3) "These dresses were low cost, as they did not require much effort to be manufactured." What is the author trying to imply with this sentence?

(A) Low-cost dresses are easier to manufacture.

(B) Cheap dresses are low in quality.

(C) Both A and B.

(D) None of the above.

(4) "These technologies were fairly simple in the beginning and included the spinning jenny, standard-sizing systems and sewing machines." Identify the rhyming words in this sentence.

(A) Technologies/fairly

(B) Systems/sewing

(C) Beginning/spinning

(D) None of the above

(5) Which of the following is a synonym of *mainstream*?

(A) Normal

(B) Conventional

(C) Ordinary

(D) All of the above

Passage 2: How to create the best environment for your pet turtle. (For questions 6 through 10)

There are various species of turtles. However, only a few can be brought home as pets. These species are relatively easy to care for at home. Two of the most commonly adopted species of turtles include red-eared turtles and box turtles.

Box turtle shells resemble a box. They are tall and dome-shaped, and that is where this species got its name. These turtles have dark skin with yellow marks all over. They grow up to six inches in length as adults.

Red-eared slider turtles are commonly known as sliders. Among all species of pet turtles, sliders are the most desirable. You will often find them at your local pet store. They are kept in swimming tanks. As babies, these turtles are four inches or even smaller in size. However, you might have to upgrade the tank as they grow older. These turtles can grow up to 11 inches in length.

There are two basic categories when it comes to a pet turtle's habitat. Some of these species are aquatic, while others are terrestrial. Box turtles are the terrestrial species of pet turtles. They naturally inhabit damp areas around the world, such as parts of the forest with moss growth. The ideal temperature for these turtles is between 75 and 85 degrees. If you live in a temperate area, it will be easier for you to keep these turtles as pets. Keep them in an outdoor enclosure with high walls and keep predators away by covering the tank with a solid lid.

People who live in colder or warm and dry climates should create an indoor area for their pet turtles. Box turtles love to dig. Therefore, make sure to cover the base of the enclosure with a lot of dirt and potting soil. You can also use scraps of carpet or shredded newspapers if soil is not available.

Box turtles also need a specific amount of moisture to survive. To create the right environment for them, add moist soil and dry, rotting leaves to the pen. Put a shoebox or a flower pot in the enclosure to provide your pet with a cozy space to hide and sleep. If you are keeping your pet turtle outdoors, never use a glass enclosure. The greenhouse effect will heat up the pen, making it hard for your pet to survive.

(6) How did box turtles get their name?

(A) They can be kept in a box.

(B) Their legs are box-shaped.

(C) Their shells are tall and dome-shaped.

(D) None of the above.

(7) Which pair of words are antonyms?

(A) Damp/dry

(B) Terrestrial/aquatic

(C) Colder/warmer

(D) All of the above

(8) Which of the following two words are synonyms?

(A) Scraps/shreds

(B) Tall/huge

(C) Both A and B

(D) None of the above

(9) What does *greenhouse effect* means?

(A) A natural process that warms the Earth's surface

(B) The process through which plants convert light into food

(C) Both A and B

(D) None of the above

(10) What is the author's intent for this passage?

(A) To inform

(B) To persuade

(C) To entertain

(D) To describe

Passage 3: The history of UFO sightings and the possibility of alien visitation on Planet Earth. (For questions 11 through 15)

If aliens ever visit Planet Earth, it will be one of the most notable events in human history. Various surveys show that over half of America's population believes aliens have visited our planet either recently or in the ancient past. The number of Americans who believe in aliens is increasing. This belief is far stronger compared to belief in the existence of ghosts and Bigfoot.

Scientists, however, do not believe in the existence of intelligent aliens. That is because there are no physical phenomena that serve as solid evidence. To prove the fact that aliens have visited this planet, a high bar is set. According to science fiction author Carl Sagan, extraordinary evidence is required to prove extraordinary claims.

UFO stands for Unidentified Flying Object. The history of UFOs is long and vague. The air force has been studying UFOs since the 1940s. In 1947, in Roswell, New Mexico, a "ground zero" for UFOs took place. Even though the Roswell incident turned out to be a crash landing of a high-altitude military balloon, it has not stopped people from believing in aliens. More UFO sightings were reported after this incident.

Americans have sighted the majority of UFOs. These sightings are less frequent in Asian and African countries despite their larger populations. What is even more surprising is that no one has ever claimed to have witnessed a UFO beyond the Canadian or Mexican borders.

The majority of UFO sightings have turned out to be regular phenomena. Most of the time, people confuse bright objects, such as meteors, fireballs and the planet Venus as UFOs. Astronomers are familiar with these objects. However, the general public fails to recognize them. Within the past decade, claims of UFO sightings have inexplicably peaked.

The majority of people who have claimed to have seen these objects are either smokers or dog walkers. According to scientists, that happens because these people spend a lot of their time outside. Most people claim to witness unidentified flying objects in the evening. These sightings have often been reported on Friday evenings when most people are drinking and relaxing.

Though some people, such as James Oberg, a former employee of NASA, have come up with conventional explanations for UFO sightings, the majority of astronomers do not believe in alien visits. However, they do believe in life beyond Earth. Therefore, they invest their time and energy into searching for the possibility of life in other star systems.

(11) Identify a synonym of *notable*.

(A) Distinguished

(B) Prominent

(C) Renowned

(D) All of the above

(12) What is the writer trying to say in the second paragraph?

(A) Aliens do not exist.

(B) Aliens have never visited Earth.

(C) The chances of alien visitation on Earth are low.

(D) There is not enough evidence to prove the existence of aliens.

(13) Which of the following words starts with a consonant?

(A) General

(B) Public

(C) Chances

(D) All of the above

(14) Identify the word that starts with a prefix.

(A) Unidentified

(B) Explicably

(C) Existence

(D) None of the above

(15) Which of the following is a compound word?

(A) Weekend

(B) Extraordinary

(C) Studying

(D) Both A & B

Passage 4: How to teach your child budgeting at an early age. (For questions 16 through 20)

Budgeting is an important life skill that everyone should acquire at an early age. Children should be taught how to budget and spend their money wisely. However, it is not as easy as it sounds. How can you convince your kids to budget their money without being boring?

You cannot expect your children to understand terms like *depositing*, *saving* and *withdrawing* in a few lessons. You can effectively communicate to them the idea of saving with visual aids. However, this requires utmost patience and careful planning.

Before you begin, know where your children think money comes from. Most children will either say the bank or an ATM. It is not an unreasonable assumption for them to make. They do not know parents work to earn the money that is then withdrawn from the bank or ATM.

You need to teach your children how money is directly related to the work you do to earn it. One of the best techniques to introduce your children to this concept is to make a chart. Add a list of chores to it and set a pay rate for each of those. Make sure these chores align with your children's age. For example, set a pay rate of 25 cents for loading the dishwasher, 50 cents for mopping the floor, 20 cents for vacuuming the carpet and so on. Increase the pay rate with an increase in the job's difficulty level.

This approach will teach your children that money does not come easy and that they have to work hard to pay for their expenses. In this way, they will learn the importance of money, and it will lay the foundation of the next stage, where you teach them to save.

Another great approach to teaching your children about the importance of money is to ask them to set goals. If they want a toy other than on Christmas or their birthday, encourage them to save for it. You can ask them to either save this amount from their pocket money or work to earn it. This will help your children estimate the amount they need to save every week to achieve the goal. For example, if they earn $2 over a week, they need $8 to buy the truck they want.

When your children are ready to save, introduce them to the three jars lesson. Get three jars and label one for money saved, the second for keeping the money to be spent and the third one for sharing. Every time you pay your children, help them with budgeting by telling them how to put money in the three jars.

(16) What did you comprehend from this reading passage?

(A) Budgeting is a life skill everyone should know.

(B) Budgeting should be taught at an early age.

(C) Teaching budgeting to your child is not easy.

(D) All of the above.

(17) Identify the pair of closest rhyming words.

(A) Saving/budgeting

(B) Depositing/withdrawing

(C) Depositing/budgeting

(D) All of the above

(18) Identify the word that starts with a prefix.

(A) Unreasonable

(B) Effectively

(C) Extraordinarily

(D) All of the above

(19) Identify the word that ends with a suffix.

(A) Directly

(B) Undeniable

(C) Unidentified

(D) None of the above

(20) Which of the following is a synonym of *assumption*?

(A) Hypothesis

(B) Supposition

(C) Best guess

(D) All of the above

Passage 5: Which factors cause acne, and is it treatable? (For questions 21 through 25)

Acne is a skin condition that can be triggered by several lifestyle features and hormonal changes. When you have acne, your skin starts to develop different types of bumps. These can appear on any part of the body, including the face, shoulders, neck and back. There are three types of acne: whiteheads, blackheads and pimples.

Various hormonal changes, such as puberty, trigger acne. Mostly, children experience acne in their teenage years. This type of hormonal acne is normal and goes away with time. It does not require any treatment. However, it may persist in those with oily skin and an unhealthy lifestyle.

Even though severe cases of acne are not harmful, they may lead to depression and low self-esteem. In other cases, acne may leave scars. Since the condition is not inherently harmful, people can choose not to treat it and embrace their skin as it is. However, if it leads to a loss of self-confidence, people with acne can buy over-the-counter treatments or prescription medicines to treat the issue.

Apart from hormonal changes, there are various other reasons why acne develops. The surface of the skin has millions of tiny pores. These pores are connected to oil glands underneath the skin. An oily liquid, known as sebum, comes out of these pores. This sebum is brought up to the skin's surface through a narrow channel referred to as a follicle.

Sebum removes the dead skin by carrying it to the surface. When these pores get clogged by oil, dead skin or bacteria, acne develops. Puberty causes oil glands to produce more oil than normal. This makes skin more prone to acne. Eating fruits, vegetables, legumes, whole grains and unprocessed foods is thought to help prevent acne from developing.

(21) What do you comprehend from this passage?

(A) Acne is a harmless skin condition that may or may not need to be treated.

(B) Hormonal and lifestyle changes can trigger acne.

(C) Certain dietary changes can relieve acne.

(D) All of the above.

(22) Which of the following is a fact?

(A) Various hormonal changes can trigger acne.

(B) If acne is causing a loss of self-confidence, over-the-counter treatments or prescription acne medicines can treat the issue.

(C) The surface of the skin has millions of tiny pores.

(D) Both A and C.

(23) What does the writer discuss in the second-to-last paragraph?

(A) Why acne develops

(B) What acne is

(C) How acne can be treated

(D) The anatomy of the skin

(24) How can acne breakouts be prevented?

(A) By applying more moisturizer

(B) With the help of weight-loss exercises

(C) By eating healthy foods

(D) None of the above

(25) "Eating fruits, vegetables, legumes, whole grains and unprocessed foods is thought to help prevent acne from developing." What does this sentence indicate when used as a context clue?

(A) Consuming unhealthy food is a cause of acne breakouts.

(B) Processed foods are healthy for the skin.

(C) Investing in inexpensive skin-care products can help with acne.

(D) None of the above.

Passage 6: Should you wish upon a shooting star? (For questions 26 through 30)

Is it possible for a shooting star to make your wish come true? It is a common belief that if you wish upon a shooting star, you will get what you wished for. Although there is no scientific evidence that proves this belief true, many people claim it is valid. Is it possible to achieve what you want by simply wishing upon a star? Before we get into this discussion, let's understand what shooting stars are.

Shooting stars are also often referred to as falling stars. However, they are not even stars to begin with. The appropriate scientific term for these falling celestial objects is meteoroids. The streaks of light in the night sky appear when meteoroids fall. Sometimes, a meteoroid is nothing but tiny bits of rock and dust. Meteor showers are very frequent. However, they are not always clearly visible. Meteors appear when the earth passes through comet debris while orbiting the sun.

There are various cultures all across the world that believe in the power of stars. In ancient times, people relied on stars to explain all sorts of things. Some cultures believe that if you wish the right way, the universe grants your wish. Whether or not this is true, if you spot a falling star, you might still be very lucky because only one in a million witness this phenomenon. So if you see one, make a wish. After all, it does not hurt to try.

Ensure that you make your wish before the meteor disappears. Close your eyes and wish for what you desire. Make sure you truly believe in what you have wished for. Do not waste your wish over a superficial desire. And do not tell anyone about your wish. Keep it a secret, and do not share it with anyone until your wish comes true.

(26) How does the writer try to hook the reader in the first paragraph?

(A) By using a question in the first line

(B) By adding quotation marks

(C) By stating a fact

(D) All of the above

(27) Which of the following is a fact?

(A) Wishing upon a shooting star will make your desires come true.

(B) Shooting stars are stars that fall from the sky.

(C) Both A and B.

(D) In ancient times, people relied on stars to explain all sorts of things.

(28) Which of the following is a synonym for *celestial*?

(A) Space

(B) Outer space

(C) Extraterrestrial

(D) All of the above

(29) What inference can readers draw from the passage?

(A) Dreams come true when you wish upon a star.

(B) There is no scientific evidence that proves dreams come true when people wish upon a star.

(C) Shooting stars are stars that fall from the sky.

(D) None of the above.

(30) "Some cultures believe that if you wish the right way, the universe grants your wish." What is this statement?

(A) A fact

(B) An opinion

(C) A truth

(D) None of the above

Test 2: Math Questions

(1) Ellen took a science test. The test was worth 500 points, and she managed to score 461.5 out of 500. What percentage did Ellen get on her science test?

(A) 92.3%

(B) 94%

(C) 46.15%

(D) 184.6%

(2) Sarah buys two rectangular plates, A and B. Plate A is 5 cm wide and 20 cm long, whereas plate B is 25 cm long. Find the width in meters of plate B provided that the areas of plates A and B are the same.

(A) 4 meters

(B) 0.04 meters

(C) 25 meters

(D) 20 meters

(3) Emily is a tall girl who wishes to get tailor-made clothes. She needs to give her measurements to the tailor. Which of the following instruments should she use to measure the exact length and width of her clothes?

(A) Meter ruler

(B) Scale

(C) Inch tape measure

(D) Centimeter ruler

(4) A teacher gave a student an equation to solve. The equation stated that $y = 8 - 3 (10^2 \div 4) + 50 - 4$. The value of y that the student obtained was 171. However, the answer was wrong. What is the correct value for y?

(A) 154

(B) 254

(C) -21

(D) 326

(5) Four out of nine people watching a certain movie are men. There are 100 more women than the men watching the movie. Calculate the total number of women in the movie theater.

(A) 500

(B) 400

(C) 900

(D) 100

(6) There are 34 people working in a restaurant. The mean age of 12 people working in the restaurant is 21 years, and the mean age of the remaining people is 32 years. What is the mean age of all 34 people working in the restaurant?

(A) 53

(B) 28

(C) 12

(D) 34

(7) A wire was in a circular shape. The diameter of the wire was 50 meters. Cooper needed to wrap that wire around a square window. Therefore, the shape of the wire was changed from circular to square. What was the length of one side of the square in centimeters?

(A) 886 centimeters

(B) 7,854 centimeters

(C) 8.86 centimeters

(D) 3,927 centimeters

(8) The length of a rectangle is 63% of its width. What is the perimeter of the rectangle when the area is 4,000 cm²?

(A) 886 centimeters

(B) 8.86 centimeters

(C) 3,925 centimeters

(D) 259.8 centimeters

(9) A survey was conducted on 100 people. They were asked about their favorite type of cake: chocolate fudge, red velvet, coffee or black forest. The following results were obtained. Which type of graph is most suitable to represent this data?

Type of cake	Number of people
Chocolate fudge	25
Red velvet	13
Coffee	54
Black forest	08

(A) Line graph

(B) Picture graph

(C) Bar graph

(D) Scatter graph

(10) The weight of 12 friends is 12 kg, 14 kg, 20 kg, 25 kg, 50 kg, 32 kg, 24 kg, 12 kg, 29 kg, 31 kg, 45 kg and xkg, respectively. If the mean weight of the 12 friends is 26 kg, what is the value of x, the mode and the median of these weights?

(A) x = 18 kg; mode = 12 kg; and median = 24.5 kg

(B) x = 12 kg; mode = 31 kg; and median = 24 kg

(C) x = 19 kg; mode = none; and median = 50 kg

(D) x = 25 kg; mode = 23 kg; and median = 25 kg

(11) The diagonal of a square playground is 450 meters long. What is the length of one side of the square in meters?

(A) 3.18 meters

(B) 10.13 meters

(C) 318.2 meters

(D) 20.25 meters

(12) If $500{,}000{,}004{,}282^0 = 1$, what is the value of $1{,}145{,}452{,}749^0$?

(A) 0

(B) 1

(C) 1,145,452,749

(D) Infinite

(13) George took a biology exam that was worth 900 points. He got a 75.6%. How many points did George manage to score in the biology exam out of 900?

(A) 707.4

(B) 700

(C) 680.4

(D) 200

(14) Jason had $50,450. He gave $450 to his son, $650 to his wife, $1,230 to his mother and $654 to his daughter. What fraction of his money did Jason give away to his family members?

(A) 1,492/25,225

(B) 373/625

(C) 2,354/50,450

(D) 4,589/38,459

(15) Emma had 34,568 pens at her shop. The mass of each pen was 450 grams. She sold 11,345 pens to another shopkeeper and 4,567 pens to a customer. What is the mass of the pens in kilograms that Emma was left with after she sold some of her pens?

(A) 8,395,200 kilograms

(B) 8,395.2 kilograms

(C) 7,160,400 kilograms

(D) 7,160.4 kilograms

(16) What is the value of x when $10^2 \times 1,000^x = 1 \div 10$?

(A) 2/3

(B) 0

(C) -3/2

(D) -1

(17) The chemist has asked Sasha to heat water up to 45 degrees. Sasha heats the water at low flame for five minutes. Which of the following measuring instruments should she use to find the temperature of the water after five minutes?

(A) Thermometer

(B) Measuring cylinder

(C) Meter ruler

(D) Water bath

(18) The teacher has asked a student to convert 6,000 years into the SI base unit of time. What unit should the student convert 6,000 years into?

(A) Milliseconds

(B) Hours

(C) Seconds

(D) Days

(19) An isosceles triangle has two 45-degree angles. Which of the following could be another name for this isosceles triangle?

(A) Scalene triangle

(B) Equilateral triangle

(C) Acute-angled triangle

(D) Right-angled triangle

(20) David was to board a flight to Houston at 4:55 a.m. The complete duration of his flight was 7 hours and 43 minutes. However, his flight got delayed by 35 minutes. At what time did David land in Houston if there was no further delay?

(A) 1:13 p.m.

(B) 1:13 a.m.

(C) 7:43 p.m.

(D) 12:00 p.m.

(21) What is the value of x when x = (1/4 + 4/7) x 28 + 23 − 35?

(A) 12

(B) 11

(C) 28

(D) 35

(22) A farmer milks eight liters of milk from a flock of sheep every day. In a week, these sheep give 56,000 milliliters of milk. How many sheep are there in the flock if the farmer gets one-fourth of the total milk from each sheep of the flock every day?

(A) 3

(B) 4

(C) 8

(D) 12

(23) Find the area of a trapezoid in m² when two of its parallel sides are 120 centimeters and 20 meters long respectively, and the height of the trapezoid is 5,000 millimeters.

(A) 53 m²

(B) 350,000 m²

(C) 530 m²

(D) 13,559 m²

(24) A lady has $10, which she wishes to divide equally among 50 children in an orphanage. She figures out that for every five children, she should keep $1. Which of the following can also be an equivalent to the fraction of money each child will get from the lady?

(A) 58/290

(B) 5/10

(C) 45/135

(D) 98/686

(25) There are 50 students in a computer class. The mean age of the students is 20. Later, five new students, all 20 years of age, and six new students, all age 35, join the class. What is the new mean age of the students in the computer class?

(A) 20

(B) 25

(C) 21.5

(D) 35

(26) If $(1/36^{-1x})$ x 1,679,616 = 7,776 ÷ 6, what is the value of x?

(A) -2

(B) 4

(C) 2

(D) 6

(27) Tom and Henry were playing cricket. Each of them got seven overs to play and no wickets to fall. Tom scored runs on 30 of the balls, whereas Henry could manage to score runs on only 17 of the balls. They could not score on the remaining balls, and they were left as dot balls. Provided that one over consists of six balls, what is the percentage of balls both Tom and Henry missed in total?

(A) 45.2%

(B) 12.5%

(C) 44%

(D) 34.7%

(28) Which of the following represent 7 x 7 x 7 x 7 x 7 x 7 x 7 x 4 9 x 7 the best?

(A) 7^{10}

(B) 7^9

(C) 343

(D) 49^4

(29) Tina has selected a circular area outside her house where she wishes to put artificial grass for decoration. The radius of the circular area is 2,500 meters. How much area in kilometers squared does she need to cover with the artificial grass?

(A) 25π/4 km²

(B) 625π km²

(C) 25,000π km²

(D) 625 km²

(30) Four hundred and fifty students were invited to participate in an online survey conducted by an ice-cream company that asked the participants about their favorite ice-cream flavor. Sixty percent of the students submitted a complete response, and 20% submitted an incomplete response. The remaining students did not participate in the survey. What is the total number of students who responded to the survey?

(A) 360

(B) 90

(C) 80

(D) 134

Test 2: Writing Questions

(1) When I was younger, I would always run away the moment someone started to discuss history, but when my mother revealed to me on a trip to China that our family descended from the Mongols, my interest was peeked.

What error can be found in the sentence above?

(A) Incorrect word usage

(B) Incorrect capitalization

(C) Incorrect comma usage

(D) incorrect verb tense

(2) In which of the following sentences is a colon not used correctly?

(A) There were only three things she liked to do on Sundays: lounge around, read a book and eat lots of delicious food.

(B) He got into the best shape of his life by doing just a few things: exercising, eating healthy and getting a good night's sleep.

(C) I have very little time to talk to you because: I have a yoga class that is starting in fifteen minutes.

(D) All of my children are in the medical field: Heston is a cardiologist; Jeanne is a pulmonologist and Deanna is a nephrologist.

(3) Blue holes in the Caribbean are made as a result of sea-level changes that take place over thousands of years, causing limestone caves to submerge; these caves, over the years, are eroded by Carbonation-Solution—the dissolving of limestone in caustic water that forms large, round sinkholes.

Which of the following errors can be found in the sentence above?

(A) Verb tense

(B) Subject-verb

(C) Incorrect capitalization

(D) Incorrect comma usage

(4) Cassidy is writing a paper for her anthropology class on the behavioral patterns of secluded populations. What kind of reference material should she use?

(A) An atlas

(B) An encyclopedia

(C) An article about secluded populations

(D) Books on the behavioral patterns of secluded populations

(5) A student has written a narrative piece that frequently uses passive voice. What is the best active voice translation of the following sentence?

"The manor was attacked by thieves, and the riches were stolen by them."

(A) The manor was attacked by thieves who stole the riches.

(B) The riches were stolen by thieves who attacked the manor.

(C) Thieves stole the riches when they attacked the manor.

(D) The thieves attacked the manor and stole the riches.

(6) When the temperature in clouds drops below $0°$ C, water and ice droplets form due to condensation and eventually grow big enough to overcome turbulence and fall to earth.

What is the simple predicate in the sentence above?

(A) Below

(B) Drops

(C) Temperature

(D) Clouds

(7) Fritha is sitting in front of her computer and thinking about the actions that her characters will take in the next few chapters of her book. She is thinking about how the novel she is writing will end. After a while, she starts writing down everything that comes to her mind. She knows some of it may not be good enough at this stage, but she thinks that she has to start somewhere.

At which step of the writing process is Fritha currently working?

(A) Revising

(B) Editing

(C) Publishing

(D) Drafting

(8) Which word is NOT spelled correctly?

A) Brigantine

B) Masonry

C) Impersonate

D) Garrolous

(9) Which of the following sentences contains a spelling or word usage error?

(A) Two siblings, Darynda and Alex, participated in the International Mathematics Olympiad and won a silver and a gold medal.

(B) Theo parked his car on the curb, leaped out of his car and ran toward the coffee shop through the heavy rain like all the demons of hell were at his heels.

(C) The boy tugged his hat down and tried his hardest to pretend to be a statue.

(D) The sagging economy had effected the whole country; prices of real estate had taken a nosedive.

(10) A 2^0 C global temperature increase would have devastating effects on the Earth: sea levels would rise as glaciers melted; four billion people would suffer from food shortages, with over 200 million at risk of floods and droughts; there would be a possible exctinction of 40% of wildlife species due to droughts and widespread climate change would reduce the agricultural capacity of many countries.

What error can be found in the sentence above?

(A) Spelling error

(B) Capitalization error

(C) Verb-tense error

(D) Subject-verb disagreement

(11) Which of the following words is not spelled correctly?

(A) Referring

(B) Trembling

(C) Ghastly

(D) Arcate

(12) An inversion layer is formed when cold air is found at the ground level while warm air is above it.

What is the simple predicate in the sentence above?

(A) Layer

(B) When

(C) Formed

(D) Found

(13) Declan Lafayette is a student of ancient languages who is learning to read and write Akkadian cuneiform script. He is writing an article about the complexity of the Akkadian language. He wants to include original examples of cuneiform script in his article.

What kind of reference material should Declan use for this purpose?

(A) An Akkadian dictionary

(B) Articles on Akkadian language

(C) Original Akkadian poems and other written works

(D) An encyclopedia on Akkadian culture

For questions 14 through 20: In the sentences below, four words are underlined and have letters underneath them. Read each sentence and choose the underlined portion that contains a grammatical, capitalization, word usage, spelling or punctuation error. **None of the sentences has more than one error.**

(14) The <u>continent</u> of Asia, with an area of over 17 billion square miles, is considerably
        A
larger <u>then</u> the continents of Australia and Africa <u>combined</u>. In fact, the landmass is so
    B   C
big that it covers 30% of the Earth's total <u>landmass</u> and is home to over 4.5 billion
                                          D
people.

(15) A mass movement, such as a <u>mudslide</u>, soil creep or <u>avalanche</u>, is any large-
                      A   B
scale movement of the Earth's surface that <u>wasn't</u> accompanied by any moving agent
                                     C
such as a river <u>or </u>an ocean wave.
              D

(16) At <u>conservative</u> plate boundaries such as the San Andreas Fault in California, plates
            A
slide past each other without <u>diverging</u> or converging and create a fault zone that is
                          B
<u>associated</u> with <u>sallow</u> earthquakes.
  C   D

(17) A global city is a city such as New York City that <u>played</u> a major
                                   A
role in global <u>affairs</u> in terms of politics, economics and culture<u>:</u> it is defined by
          B   C
influence rather than size; it can help set global trends; and it is the driver of <u>economic</u>
                                                              D
growth for a country.

(18) The oceanic swirl of currents, or <u>gyre,</u> determines the temperature of coastal areas in
                                             A
the Southern and Northern Hemispheres<u>;</u> coastal areas are cooler because cold oceanic

                                              B
currents <u>advect</u> water from the poles toward the equator. The resulting <u>upweling</u>
          C   D
currents cool the area down.

(19) Food security<u>, in essence,</u> means that all people at all times within their lives have
                        A
access to enough <u>nutricious</u> food in order to maintain an active and healthy life;
                        B
some countries <u>produce</u> a food surplus or have enough financial
                        C
resources to buy enough food<u>, whereas</u> other countries are food deficient and may not
                                D
have the financial resources to buy food from elsewhere.

(20) By 1914, the United States, after <u>whethering</u> many storms, <u>had</u> emerged as a
                                            A   B
strong and <u>prosperous</u> regional power in the Northern Hemisphere with a <u>widening</u>
                C   D
influence over financial markets throughout the world.

For questions 21 through 24: The following short essay was written by Kelsie, an aspiring geologist, as a school assignment.

Types of Desert Landscapes: Erg, Reg, Hamada and Desert Pavement

By Kelsie Mark

(1) There are many types of desert landscapes. (2) They are erg, reg, hamada and desert pavement. (3) These desert landscapes are created by selective deflation—the erosion of loose material by wind. (4) Erg deserts are the classic sandy deserts that are usually seen in movies with glowing golden sand and shifting dunes. (5) Reg deserts are gravelly or stony deserts created by the deposition of the fine, whittled load. (6) The hamada desert is barren, bereft of sand because the winds have blown all loose material away. (7) It is made of large areas of flat, naked rock faces with giant weathered rocks casually strewn about the landscape. (8) Wind erosion only takes place when the wind is loaded with loose material such as sand or pebbles. (9) Desert pavement is a surface of smooth interlocked pebbles or gravel worn flat by wind erosion over hundreds of years.

(21) Kelsie wants to join sentences 1 and 2 together to create an introductory sentence that is clear, concise, logical and grammatically correct. Which of the following most effectively combines sentences 1 and 2?

(A) There are many types of desert landscapes, they are erg, reg, hamada and desert pavement.

(B) There are many types of desert landscapes, such as erg, reg, hamada and desert pavement.

(C) Erg, reg and desert pavement are some types of desert landscapes.

(D) There are many types of desert landscapes; erg, reg, hamada and desert pavement.

(22) After rereading the short essay, Kelsie realizes that she should connect sentences 6 and 7 because sentence 7 continues the explanation of what a hamada desert is.

What transition word, conjunction or punctuation mark should she choose to connect these sentences?

The Hamada desert is barren, bereft of sand because the winds have blown all loose material away. It is made of large areas of flat, naked rock faces with giant weathered rocks casually strewn about the area.

(A) Semicolon

(B) And

(C) Comma

(D) Yet

(23) One of Kelsie's classmates reviewed her essay and told her that she should add a concluding sentence at the end of the essay. Kelsie decides that she wants to conclude the essay with a statement that summarizes the essay and talks about the time it takes for these landscapes to form. She wants to maintain the tone and style of her essay.

Which of the following best accomplishes this goal?

(A) The shaping of these landscapes took centuries, with some taking hundreds of thousands of years to form.

(B) All these landscapes formed over hundreds to thousands of years.

(C) Over millennia, these landscapes took shape.

(D) All of these landscapes were formed by wind erosion over thousands of years. Some of them even predate human civilization.

(24) Kelsie is considering deleting this sentence to tighten the essay and to remove extra words: "Wind erosion only takes place when the wind is loaded with loose material such as sand or pebbles."

Should Kelsie delete this sentence?

(A) Yes, because the sentence reiterates information that is already mentioned elsewhere in the essay.

(B) No, because the sentence helps develop the essay's main topic and adds more information.

(C) Yes, because the sentence is not relevant to the ideas presented in the previous sentences and is jarring to read at this point.

(D) No, because the sentence effectively connects the ideas mentioned in the preceding sentence to the ideas mentioned in the succeeding sentences.

For questions 25 through 27: The following introductions were written by five students.

I. For more than 5,000 years, ancient civilizations like the Egyptians, Romans, Mesopotamians and Akkadians ruled over the earth. An unsurprising similarity among all these civilizations is that each one had a government with one main ruler.

II. Before the advent of airplanes, it took months for a person to travel across long distances, so some people never went far from their homes.

III. As technology has advanced, phones have become not just a medium for contacting someone. Rather, they have become a constant source of distraction. With all the games, music and videos just a tap away, children pay more attention to their phones than their studies. Cell phones have become a hindrance. They are a source of increased disruption in classrooms. Therefore, the use of cell phones should be banned in classrooms.

IV. The difference between betraying a trust and gossiping is not much; one slip, and you are done. Talking is a natural part of life; it is a societal norm.

V. Charging a premium while offering low-quality products is wrong. In the three years I've worked as a tutor, I've come across children whose parents got them the best tutors their money could buy, only to be disappointed again and again.

(25) Which of the following introductions is most likely to be used in an argumentative essay?

(A) I

(B) II

(C) III

(D) V

(26) Which of the following introductions is most likely to be found at the beginning of a compare-and-contrast essay?

(A) I

(B) II

(C) IV

(D) V

(27) Which of the following sentences is most likely to be found at the start of a speech given by a young, experienced tutor?

(A) II

(B) III

(C) IV

(D) V

For questions 28 through 30: The following questions are based on the following unfinished outline.

For her assignment, Nona must write about the job she wants to do when she graduates. She wants to write a short descriptive essay about the tasks a real estate agent performs. But before she starts writing, Nona has to assemble her research into an outline.

The Life of a Real Estate Agent

1. Daily tasks

A. Finish administrative tasks

    1. File documents, make copies

    2. Handle phone calls

    3. Prepare purchase agreements, rental agreements, deeds or other documents

    4. Review purchase contracts.

B. Complete any outbound tasks

    1. Show properties to potential buyers or renters

    2. View local properties

    3. Attend home inspections/appraisals.

C. _____

    1. Manage property listings

    2. Update property listings

    3. Take listing photos

    4. Facilitate meetings between buyers and sellers

    5. Research market trends.

2. Client-related responsibilities

A. Seek information from clients

    1. Identify clients' needs or preferences

    2. Discuss financial ability

    3. Negotiate contracts; research properties that meet the clients' requirements.

B. Provide guidance to clients

    1. Instruct clients about market prices, legal requirements and conditions

    2. Help clients negotiate with buyers or sellers

    3. Assist buyers in purchasing a property

    4. Assist sellers in marketing their property.

3. _____

A. Market property to the public

    1. Write listing descriptions

    2. Advertise property

    3. Create and print brochures, postcards and flyers.

B. Market yourself

    1. Build an online presence

    2. Manage lead response

    3. Follow up on leads

    4. Advertise in any way possible.

(28) Which of the following titles should Nona put into the heading 3C blank?

(A) Miscellaneous tasks

(B) Some other tasks

(C) Agency tasks

(D) Client work

(29) Nona has left heading 1C blank. Which of the following titles should she put into the blank?

(A) Advertise the real estate agency

(B) Learning how to advertise

(C) Marketing

(D) How to market yourself

(30) Finally, Nona is done with her outline and wants to write the first sentence or two of her essay. She wants to give a condensed review of what the job of a real estate agent is like.

Which of the following best accomplishes this goal?

(A) Out of the many career choices available to me, I chose to become a real estate agent because I find it exciting to talk to people.

(B) Real estate agents are chameleons—they negotiate, manage and market themselves without a moment lost.

(C) A real estate agent's job is an amalgamation of several contrasting jobs. They never have a free day to themselves.

(D) Real estate agents are salespeople, advisers, negotiators, researchers and managers: they are jacks of all trades.

Essay Question:

Describe The Most Vivid Experience of Your Life.

Test 2: Reading Answers & Explanations

(1) (A) Industrialization, industry, of, use.

Vowels include *a, e, i, o* and *u. An* is placed before words that start with a vowel. In the first paragraph, various words start with vowels. These include *industrialization, industry, of* and *use.*

(2) (B) Quality/quantity.

Antonyms are a pair of words that have opposite meanings. In the second paragraph, *quality* and *quantity* are two words that are opposite to one another. *Quality* means "worth, value or class of an object." On the contrary, *quantity* is "the amount, number or measure of an object or objects."

(3) (B) Cheap dresses are low in quality.

Sometimes authors do not directly state an idea. They use context clues for the readers to understand or interpret what they are trying to say. This author has written this sentence to urge readers to come up with a conclusion of their own. The author does not directly say that cheap dresses are low quality. However, the writer says, "These dresses were low cost, as they did not require much effort to be manufactured" to indirectly communicate the message to readers.

(4) (C) Beginning/spinning.

"These technologies were fairly simple in the beginning and included the spinning jenny, standard-sizing systems and sewing machines." There are two words that rhyme with each other in this sentence—*beginning* and *spinning*. Rhyming words are words that end with the same sound.

(5) (D) All of the above.

There are various synonyms of the word *mainstream*. Some of them include *normal, conventional* and *ordinary. Mainstream* refers to common phenomena.

(6) (C) Their shells are tall and dome-shaped.

According to this passage, box turtles got their name from the shape of their shell. Their shells are tall and dome-shaped, appearing like a box.

(7) (D) All of the above.

Antonyms have opposite meanings. Damp/dry, terrestrial/aquatic and colder/warmer are all antonyms.

(8) (A) Scraps/shreds.

Synonyms are words that have the same or similar meaning. *Scraps* and *shreds* both mean "leftover bits and pieces."

(9) (A) A natural process that warms the earth's surface.

According to the dictionary, the greenhouse effect is a natural phenomenon that warms the earth's surface. It is why the rapidly increasing temperature of the earth is also referred to as global warming.

(10) (A) To inform.

In this passage, the author intends to inform the readers on how to care for a pet turtle. It is written for those who are interested in learning how to create a favorable environment for their pet.

(11) (D) All of the above.

Notable can be replaced with various synonyms, including *distinguished*, *prominent* and *renowned*.

(12) (D) There is not enough evidence to prove the existence of aliens.

The writer starts the second paragraph by saying that scientists do not believe in the existence of intelligent aliens. However, the writer does not say that scientists disapprove of alien existence. The author is trying to say scientists do believe in the possibilities of alien existence. However, scientists do not believe them to be smart enough to visit planet Earth.

(13) (D) All of the above.

Consonants are all English letters that are not *a, e, i, o* and *u*. Unlike vowels, consonants are preceded by *a* instead of *an*. All answer options for this question start with a consonant.

(14) (A) Unidentified.

The part that comes before the root word, that changes its meaning, is a prefix. In the word *unidentified, un-* is the prefix. The root word *identified* makes sense even when the prefix is removed.

(15) (D) Both A and B.

When two complete words are joined to form one long word, a compound word is formed. In this question, there are two options that are compound words: *weekend* and *extraordinary*. When we break *weekend* into two shorter words, we get *week* and *end*. When we break *extraordinary* into two smaller words, we get *extra* and *ordinary*.

(16) (D) All of the above.

In this passage, the writer is trying to highlight the importance of teaching children how to budget at an early age. According to the writer, budgeting is an important life skill everyone should know. However, developing this skill in children isn't easy. It requires patience and proper planning.

(17) (C) Depositing/budgeting.

Rhyming words are different words that end with the same sound. You will often come across such word relationships in poetry or poetic prose. *Depositing* and *budgeting* end with the same sound—*ting*. Therefore, they rhyme with one another.

(18) (A) Unreasonable.

The part that comes before a root word and changes its meaning is known as a prefix. The root word makes sense even if the prefix is removed. *Unreasonable* starts with a prefix. If you remove *un-* from the root word, the word *reasonable* still makes sense.

(19) (A) Directly.

A suffix is added to the end of a word. The root word still makes sense even when the suffix is removed. *Directly* ends with a suffix. If you remove *-ly*, the word still makes sense.

(20) (D) All of the above.

Hypothesis, supposition and *best guess* are all synonyms of *assumption*.

(21) (D) All of the above.

In this passage, the author explains what acne is and what causes it to develop. It is a harmless skin condition that may or may not need to be treated. Acne is often triggered by hormonal and lifestyle changes. Healthy dietary changes can prevent acne to a certain extent.

(22) (D) Both A and C.

A fact is a statement that can be proven with evidence. Both Options A and C are facts, as they have been proven with scientific research.

(23) (D) The anatomy of the skin.

In the second-to-last paragraph, the writer explains the anatomy of skin in an attempt to educate readers about what causes acne.

(24) (C) By eating healthy foods.

According to the last paragraph, acne may be naturally prevented with the consumption of healthy foods.

(25) (A) Consuming unhealthy food is the cause of acne breakouts.

This line indicates that eating unhealthy food can cause acne breakouts. The writer does not directly state the point but rather uses context clues to indirectly convey the message to the audience.

(26) (A) By using a question in the first line.

Writers use various techniques to hook the readers. This writer starts this passage with a question to hook the reader.

(27) (D) In ancient times, people relied on stars to explain all sorts of things.

Facts are statements that have been proven valid and are supported with evidence. Option D is a fact. It is supported by evidence that can be found in historical documents.

(28) (D) All of the above.

Space, outer space and extraterrestrial are all synonyms of *celestial.*

(29) (B) There is no scientific evidence that proves dreams come true when people wish upon a star.

In this passage, the writer is explaining how some people believe that their desires can come true by wishing upon a star. However, the intent of the passage is clearly for readers to infer that there is no scientific evidence that proves this claim to be true.

(30) (B) An opinion.

Opinions are personal statements. They are not necessarily accepted by society, and they are not supported by scientific evidence. This statement is an opinion, as there is no scientific evidence that proves that if you wish the right way, the universe will grant your wish.

Test 2: Math Answers & Explanations

(1) (A) 92.3%.

To calculate the percentage, the formula is:

Percentage = points obtained/total points

Substitute the values of the points obtained by Ellen and the test's total points in the formula.

Percentage obtained = 461.5/500

Percentage obtained = 92.3%.

(2) (B) 0.04 meters.

Since the answer is required in meters, convert the measurements.

1 centimeter = 1/100 meters

Therefore, the length of rectangle A = 20/100 = 0.2 meters.

The width of rectangle A = 5/100 = 0.05 meters

The length of rectangle B = 25/100 = 0.25 meters

The formula for the area of a rectangle is:

Area = length x width.

Calculate the area of rectangle A by substituting the values of length and width in the formula.

Area of rectangle A = 0.2 x 0.05 = 0.01 m²

Since the area of rectangle A = area of rectangle B, the area of rectangle B is also 0.01 m².

To calculate the width of rectangle B, substitute the value of the area and the length in the formula for the area of the rectangle.

0.01 = 0.25 x width of rectangle B

Divide 0.01 by 0.25 to obtain the width of rectangle B.

Width of rectangle B = 0.04 meters.

(3) (C) Inch tape measure.

Apart from an inch tape, a centimeter ruler and meter ruler are also instruments to measure lengths. However, they are less precise and are mostly suitable for measuring smaller lengths, unlike an inch tape. The scale can only be used to measure masses of objects, not lengths.

(4) (C) -21.

Apply PEMDAS.

First, open the parentheses by dividing 10^2 by 4.

$10^2 = 100$

$100/4 = 25$

$y = 8 - 3\ (25) + 50\ -4$

Multiply 3 by 25 to obtain 75.

$y = 8 - 75 + 50 - 4$

Now, add 50 to -75 to obtain -25. When adding a negative and a positive number, the answer will get the sign of the number that is bigger. In this case, -75 is the bigger number, so the answer will get the negative sign.

$y = 8 - 25 - 4.$

Then add 8 to -20 to obtain -17.

$y = -17 - 4$

Lastly, subtract -4 from -17. When a term with a minus sign is subtracted from another number with a minus sign, the two numbers add up.

Therefore, $- 17 - -4 = -21.$

The student obtained the wrong value of y because he followed the following wrong order of operations:

He first subtracted 3 from 8 to obtain 5.

$y = 5 (10^2 \div 4) + 50 - 4$

He then solved the parentheses and multiplied 5 by 25 to obtain 125.

$y = 125 + 50 - 4$

The student then added 50 to 125 to obtain 175 and subtracted 4 from 175 to obtain 171 as the incorrect final answer.

(5) (A) 500.

Let the total number of people watching the film be x.

The total number of men watching the film will then be 4/9 (x).

The total number of women watching the film will be 4/9(x) + 100 because there are 100 more women than men present.

Create an equation from the data provided.

4/9(x) + 4/9(x) + 100 = x

Take 9 as the LCM on the left-hand side to make the denominator the same for each fraction.

4/9(x) + 4/9(x) + 900/9 = x.

Remove the denominator by multiplying 9 with x on the right-hand side.

4x + 4x + 900 = 9x.

Add the two 4xs to obtain 8x and then subtract from 9x to obtain the value of x, which is 900.

x = 900

There are 900 people watching the film.

Since 4/9 of the total people are men:

4/9 (900) = 400. There are 400 men watching the film.

As there are 100 more women than the men, the total number of women present in the theater is 500.

(6) (B) 28.

The mean value is the average value of the data.

The formula for calculating the mean is:

Mean = sum of data/total number of data

For the first 12 people, the mean age is 21 years. The sum of their ages, x, can be calculated by substituting these values in the formula for mean.

21 = x/12

The sum of their ages is 21 x 12 = 252

For the remaining 34 − 12 = 22 people, the mean age is 32 years. The sum of their ages, y, can be calculated by substituting these values in the formula for mean.

32 = y/22

The sum of their ages is 32 x 22 = 704

For all 34 people, the sum of their ages is 252 + 704 = 956.

To calculate the mean for 34 people, substitute the values in the formula.

Mean = 956/34 = 28 years.

(7) (D) 3,927 centimeters.

Since the final answer is required in centimeters, convert the measurements.

1 meter = 100 centimeters

Therefore, 50 meters = 50 x 100 = 5,000 centimeters.

The radius of the circle is diameter/2 = 5,000/2 = 2,500 centimeters.

The perimeter/circumference of the circle = $2\pi r = 2\pi(2,500) = 5,000\pi$ centimeters.

Since the circular wire is then folded into a squared wire, the perimeter will remain the same.

The perimeter of a square = 4L.

Substitute the value of the circumference of the circle in the perimeter of a square and divide it by 4 to obtain the value of the length of one side of the square.

$5,000\pi/4 = L = 3,926.9$ centimeters. This value is approximately 3,927 centimeters.

(8) (D) 259.8 centimeters.

Let the width of the rectangle be x.

To remove the percentage sign, divide 63% by 100 to obtain 63/100.

Since the length of the rectangle is 63% of the width, length = 63/100(x).

Area of the rectangle = length x width.

Substitute the value of area and the expressions for length and width in the formula.

4000 = 63/100(x) (x)

Multiply 100 by 4,000 to remove the denominator from the right-hand side and multiply the two xs to obtain x^2.

$400,000 = 63x^2$.

Divide 400,000 by 63 and take the square of the obtained value to get the two values of x.

$\sqrt{(400,000/63)} = x = \pm 79.7$

Only take the positive value of x because lengths can never be negative.

The width, x, of the rectangle is 79.7 centimeters.

The length of the rectangle, 63/100(x) = 63/100(79.7) = 50.2 centimeters.

The perimeter of the rectangle = 2(length) + 2(width)

Perimeter = 2(79.7) + 2(50.2)

Perimeter = 259.8 centimeters.

(9) (C) Bar graph.

In this data, a comparison is being drawn between the numbers of people who like each type of cake. Therefore, a bar graph is the most suitable form of representation for drawing comparisons between different groups.

(10) (A) x = 18 kg; mode = 12 kg; and median = 24.5 kg.

Mean is the average value of the data.

The formula for calculating mean is:

Mean = sum of data/total number of data

The sum of the weights is 12 + 14 + 20 + 25 + 50 + 32 + 24 + 12 + 29 + 31 + 45 + x = 294 + x. The total is 12.

Substitute the values in the formula to obtain the value of x.

26 = 294 + x/12.

Multiply 12 by 26 to obtain 312.

Subtract 294 from 312 to obtain the value of x.

312 − 294 = x = 18

The mode is the most frequently occurring and the most repeated value of the data. In this set of values, 12 years is repeated two times and more than any other age. Therefore, the mode is 12 years.

The median is a set of data's middle value.

To calculate the median of the data, first arrange the set of values in ascending order.

12, 12, 14, 18, 20, 24, 25, 29, 31, 32, 45, 50 is the new order.

When the total number of data is an even number, such as 12 in this case, there are two middle values.

The two middle values in this data are 24 and 25 years.

The median can be calculated by adding the two middle values and dividing the sum by 2.

$24 + 25 = 49/2 = 24.5$ years is the median age.

(11) (C) 318.2 meters.

In a square, all four sides are equal. Let the length of one side of the square be x.

The diagonal of the square is 450 meters long. To obtain the value of x, use the Pythagorean theorem.

The diagonal is the hypotenuse.

$Hypotenuse^2 = base^2 + perpendicular^2$

$450^2 = x^2 + x^2$

$202{,}500 = 2x^2$

Divide 205,200 by x and take the root of the obtained value to find the two values of x.

$\sqrt{(202{,}500/2)} = x = \pm 318.2$

Since the length of a square can never be negative, the negative value of x will be ignored.

Hence, the length of a square with diagonal 450 meters is 318.2 meters.

(12) (B) 1.

Any term with 0 in its power is equal to 1, no matter how large or small the number may be.

(13) (C) 680.4.

The formula for obtaining percentage:

Percentage = points obtained/total points.

Let the points obtained by George in biology be x.

Substitute the values given in the data in the formula for calculating percentage.

75.6% = x/900

Remove the % sign from 75.6% by dividing it by 100 to obtain 75.6/100.

Multiply 900 by 75.6/100 to obtain the value of x.

x = (75.6/100) x 900 = 680.4 points that George scored on his exam.

(14) (A) 1,492/25,225.

Add up the amount of money Jason gave to his family members.

$450 + $650 + $1,230 + $654 = $2,984.

He gave $2,984 out of $50,450 to his family. The fractional representation of this information is 2,984/50,450.

Both 2,984/50,450 are further divisible by 2.

2,984 divided by 2 is 1,492, and 50,450 divided by 2 is 25,225.

Hence, the simplified fraction of the amount of money Jason gave to his family members is 1,492/25,225.

(15) (B) 8,395.2 kilograms.

To find the total number of pens Emma sold, add up the pens she sold to the two people.

11,345 + 4,567 = 15,912 pens

To find the number of pens she is left with, subtract 15,912 from 34,568 to obtain 18,656 pens.

The mass of each pen is 450 grams.

Therefore, the mass of 18,656 pens will be 18,656 x 450 = 8,395,200 grams.

Convert the mass in grams to kilograms to calculate the final answer.

1 gram = 1/1,000 kilograms.

Hence, 8,395,200 grams = 8,395,200/1,000 = 8,395.2 kilograms of pens.

(16) (D) -1.

First, convert the entire equation into the same base, which is 10 in this case.

1,000 can be written as 10 x 10 x 10, and 10 x 10 x 10 can be written as 10^3.

1 can also be written as 10^0 because any term with power zero is equal to one.

10 can also be written as 10^1 because if a term does not have any power, the power is 1.

Hence, the new equation with terms in base 10 is 10^2 x $(10^3)^x = 10^0 \div 10^1$.

Taking the left-hand side, when the bases are the same and the terms are multiplied, their powers add up.

Taking the right-hand side, when the bases are the same and the terms are divided, their powers get subtracted from each other.

Hence, the equation can now also be written as $10^{2+3x} = 10^{0-1}$.

When the terms have the same base on both sides of the = sign, their powers are also equal.

So, 2 + 3x = 0 − 1

Subtract 2 from -1 to obtain -3 on the right-hand side.

3x = -3

Divide -3 by 3 to obtain -1 as the value of x.

(17) (A) Thermometer.

A measuring cylinder is used to measure the volume of liquids. A meter ruler is used to measure the length, and a water bath is not a measuring instrument. A thermometer is used for measuring temperatures.

(18) (C) Seconds.

There are seven base quantities from which other quantities are derived. One of these seven quantities is time. Although it can be measured in several other units like hours, days, milliseconds and months, the standard SI base unit for time is seconds.

(19) (D) Right-angled triangle.

If a triangle is an isosceles, it means that two of the three sides and angles of that triangle are equal. If one of the angles in an isosceles triangle is 45 degrees, there will be one more side with the same angle.

The sum of the interior angles of the triangle is 180 degrees.

Let the value of the third angle be x.

To find the third angle, subtract these two 45-degree angles from 180.

45 + 45 + x = 180

x = 180 − 45- 45

x = 90 degrees

The third angle of this triangle is 90 degrees. If a triangle has one 90-degree angle, it is called a right-angled triangle.

(20) (A) 1:13 p.m.

David was to board a flight at 4:55 a.m., but since his flight was delayed by 35 minutes, he boarded 35 minutes late.

There are 60 minutes in an hour. So, if 5 minutes out of 35 minutes are added to 4:55, the time will be 5:00 a.m. After adding the remaining 30 minutes, the clock will show 5:30 a.m., and David boarded the flight at 5:30 a.m.

The duration of the flight was 7 hours and 43 minutes.

If you add 7 hours to 5 hours, you get 12:30. However, after the clock strikes 12, a.m. changes into p.m. The time after 7 hours have passed is 12:30 p.m.

Since there are 60 minutes in an hour, if you add 30 more minutes out of the remaining 43 minutes of the flight at 12:30 p.m., the time will be 1:00 p.m. After adding the remaining 13 minutes, David will land in Houston at 1:13 p.m.

(21) (B) 11.

Apply PEMDAS.

First, open the parentheses by adding 1/4 and 4/7 to obtain 23/28.

Then multiply 23/28 with 28 to obtain 23.

Add 23 to 23 to obtain 46.

Lastly, subtract 35 from 46 to obtain 11 as x.

(22) (B) 4.

If the flock of sheep gives eight liters of milk each day and each sheep in the flock gives one-fourth of the total milk each day, each sheep in the flock gives (1/4)(8) = 2 liters.

Let the number of sheep be x.

x = 8/2 = 4 sheep

There are four sheep in the flock.

(23) (A) 53 m².

Since the answer is required in m², convert all the measurements into meters.

1 cm = 1/100 meters

Hence, 120 cm = 120/100 = 1.2 meters

Similarly, 1 mm = 1/1,000 meters

So, 5,000 mm = 5,000/1,000 = 5 meters

The trapezoid height is five meters, and the lengths of the two parallel sides are 1.2 meters and 20 meters respectively. Substitute these values in the formula for the area of the trapezoid.

Area of trapezoid = 1/2 (height) (sum of parallel sides)

Area of trapezoid = 1/2 (5) (1.2 + 20)

Area of trapezoid = 53 m².

(24) (A) 58/290.

For 5/10: Both 5 and 10 are divisible by 5. 5 divided by 5 is equal to 1, and 10 divided by 5 is equal to 2. So, the simplified form of 5/10 is 1/2.

For 45/135: Both 45 and 135 are divisible by 45. 45 divided by 45 is equal to 1, and 135 divided by 45 is equal to 3. So, the simplified form of 45/135 is 1/3.

For 98/686: Both 98 and 686 are divisible by 98. 98 divided by 98 is equal to 1, and 686 divided by 98 is equal to 7. So, the simplified form of 98/686 is 1/7.

And for 58/290: Both 58 and 290 are divisible by 58. 58 divided by 58 is equal to 1, and 290 divided by 58 is equal to 5. Hence, the simplified form of 58/290 is 1/5.

(25) (C) 21.5.

Mean is the average of the data.

The formula for calculating mean is:

Mean = sum of data/total number of data

Let the sum of ages be x.

Substitute the value of mean and the total number of ages to calculate the sum of ages for 50 students.

$20 = x/50$

Multiply 20 by 50 to obtain 1,000 as the value of x.

Eleven new students are added to 50 students to give a new total of 61 students.

The new sum of ages is $1,000 + 5(20) + 6(35) = 1,310$.

Hence, the new mean = $1,310/61 = 21.5$ years.

(26) (A) -2.

$1/36^{-1x}$ can be written as 36^{1x}.

First, convert the entire equation into terms with the same base, which is 6.

36 can be written as 6 x 6, and 6 x 6 can be written as 6^2. Hence, 36^x can be written as 6^{2x}.

1,679,616 can be written as 6 x 6 x 6 x 6 x 6 x 6 x 6 x 6, and this can be written as 6^8.

7,776 can be written as 6 x 6 x 6 x 6 x 6, and this can be written as 6^5.

6 can be written as 6^1 because a number that has no power has 1 as its power.

Hence, the new equation will be $6^{2x} \times 6^8 = 6^5 \div 6^1$.

Taking the left-hand side, when the bases of the terms are the same and the terms are multiplied, their powers add up.

Taking the right-hand side, when the bases of the terms are the same and the terms are divided, their powers are subtracted from each other.

Hence, the new form of the equation will be $6^{2x + 8} = 6^{5 - 1}$.

If the bases of the terms on each side of the = sign are the same, their powers are equal.

So, $2x + 8 = 5 - 1$.

$2x + 8 = 4$

Subtract 8 from 4 to obtain -4.

$2x = -4$

Divide -4 by 2 to obtain -2 as the value of x.

(27) (C) 44%.

One over consists of 6 balls.

Therefore, seven overs consist of 7 x 6 = 42 balls. Both Tom and Henry got to play 42 balls each.

Tom missed 42 – 30 = 12 balls, and Henry missed 42 – 17 = 25 balls.

In total, both Tom and Henry missed 25 + 12 = 37 balls.

Both Tom and Henry faced 42 + 42 = 84 balls.

Percentage of missed balls = (number of balls missed/total number of balls faced) x 100

Percentage of missed balls = (37/84) x 100

Percentage of missed balls = 44%.

(28) (A) 7^{10}.

49 can be written as 7 x 7, and 7 x 7 can be written as 7^2.

Hence, 7 x 7 x 7 x 7 x 7 x 7 x 7 x 4 9 x 7 can be written as 7 x 7 x 7 x 7 x 7 x 7 x 7 x 7 x 7 x 7, and this can be written as 7^{10}.

(29) (A) $25\pi/4$ kilometers^2.

Since the answer is required in kilometers, convert the measurements.

1 meter = 1/1,000 kilometers

Hence, the radius of the circle = 2,500/1,000 = 2.5 kilometers.

Area of circle = πr^2

Area of circle = $\pi(2.5)^2$

Area of circle = $25\pi/4$ kilometers^2.

(30) (A) 360.

To find the number of students who responded completely to the survey, first remove the % sign from 60% by dividing it by 100 and obtaining 60/100.

The number of students who responded completely to the survey = (60/100) x 450 = 270 students.

To find the number of students who responded incompletely to the survey, remove the % sign from 20% by dividing it by 100 and obtaining 20/100.

The number of students who incompletely responded to the survey = (20/100) x 450 = 90 students.

270 + 90 = 360 students responded to the survey either completely or incompletely.

Test 2: Writing Answers & Explanations

(1) (A) Incorrect word usage.

A word usage error is at the very end of the sentence. The word *peeked* means "to have looked at something or someone quickly or sneakily." In this sentence, the use of this word makes no sense. Instead, the word *piqued* should have been used. *Piqued* means "roused/stimulated interest or curiosity in something." This meaning is appropriate for the context of a paragraph where a character's interest is *piqued*.

(2) (C) I have very little time to talk to you because: I have a yoga class that is starting in fifteen minutes.

As a rule, a colon is used to introduce something. A colon should always follow an independent clause. The colon can introduce a list, highlight the succeeding clause or emphasize the clause. In the first option, the colon is appropriately used just after the clause to introduce a list. In Option B, the writer has appropriately chosen to use a comma to introduce a list, but in Option C the writer has incorrectly used a colon after the subordinating conjunction *because* to join an independent and a dependent clause together. This is incorrect. A colon should never be used with a conjunction.

(3) (C) Incorrect capitalization.

There are capitalization errors in this passage. *Carbonation-Solution* is not a proper noun. Thus, it should not be capitalized.

(4) (D) Books on the behavioral patterns of secluded populations.

Cassidy is writing an essay on the behavioral patterns of secluded populations. To make sure her work contains facts rather than opinions or disapproved theories, it would be best if she read some books on behavioral patterns of secluded populations.

(5) (D) The thieves attacked the manor and stole the riches.

Passive voice is when an action is done *to* the subject of the sentence. Active voice is when an action is done *by* the subject. In the given sentence, the subject is being acted upon. Option A is incorrect because it does not change the passive sentence to active. In Option B, part of the sentence is active while the rest remains passive. Option C could be correct, but it changes the original sentence too much. In this option, the subordinating conjunction *when* is used instead of the coordinating conjunction *and*. This leaves Option D. In Option D, the sentence is translated directly into active voice without any new additions. Thus, Option D is correct.

(6) (B) Drops.

The verb *drops* is the simple predicate in this sentence. The simple predicate is the verb that tells the reader what the subject is doing in a sentence. In this case, the simple predicate *drops* tells us the effects of the subject *temperature* in this sentence.

(7) (D) Drafting.

Fritha is currently writing whatever comes to mind. She cannot be revising her work because it is mentioned in the question that she is "writing down everything." When work is revised, words are added or deleted, paragraphs are shifted from their places and prose is revised. She cannot be editing because during editing, the work is checked for pacing errors, continuity errors, plot fluidity and typing errors. She can also not be publishing her work because publishing requires a completely edited work. Thus, Fritha can only be drafting her work.

(8) (D) Garrolous.

In the four choices presented, *garrolous* is spelled incorrectly. It should be written as *garrulous*.

(9) (D) The sagging economy had effected the whole country; prices of real estate had taken a nosedive.

Options A, B and C do not have any errors. However, in Option D, the word *effected* is used instead of the word *affected* as the sentence's simple predicate. *Effect* and *affect* are words that sound similar; they are homophones. *Effect* is the end result of a cause, whereas *affect*—used as a verb in this sentence—means that something influences or changes something.

(10) (A) Spelling error.

The word *exctinction* is misspelled in this paragraph. It should be written as *extinction*.

(11) (D) Arcate.

Arcate is spelled incorrectly. It should be written as *arcuate*.

(12) (C) Formed.

The simple predicate is the verb that tells the reader what the subject is doing or what action a subject is taking. The simple predicate usually comes after the subject. In this case, the predicate is *formed* because it comes after the subject *inversion layer*. Thus, Option C is correct.

(13) (C) Original Akkadian poems and other written works.

Declan is writing an article about the Akkadian language's complexity and wants to include original examples of cuneiform script in his article. In this case, an Akkadian dictionary would not be the best option, as it would not provide him with original examples of cuneiform script. Similarly, other articles based on the Akkadian language would not provide him with what he wants. An encyclopedia—a secondary resource—written on Akkadian culture is irrelevant to his goal; he is focusing on cuneiform, not culture. Thus, Declan would need to use original Akkadian poems and other written words to cite original cuneiform script examples in his article.

(14) (B) then.

The word *then* is used incorrectly in this sentence. *Then* shows an action that takes place in relation to time (to show what comes next or what used to be). For example, "Bianca completed an HIIT workout, then she completed a resistance training circuit." The word *than* is used to make a comparison between two things. *Then* and *than* are homophones—words that sound alike.

In this case, *than* should be used because a comparison is being made between Asia's continent and the continents of Australia and Africa.

(15) (C) wasn't.

In this sentence, the past form *wasn't* of the verb *is* is used instead of the present form. The whole sentence is written in the present tense, as shown by the use of the verb *is*. Option C is the past tense *wasn't*. This verb does not agree with the tense and is incorrect.

(16) (D) sallow.

Sallow means that someone has a wan and pale complexion that looks yellow, while *shallow* means something that has very little depth. In this case, the word *shallow* should be used to describe the low depth of earthquakes.

(17) (A) played.

In this sentence, there is a verb-tense error. The sentence is written in the present tense as indicated by the presence of the present-tense verb *is*, but the verb *played* is a past-tense verb. It does not agree with the tense of the sentence.

(18) (D) upweling.

Four words are underlined in this sentence. The first word contains no error. The semicolon in Option B is correctly used, as it connects the two sentences. The word *advect* is correctly used to show the bulk movement of a liquid. This leaves Option D. The word *upweling* is misspelled. It should be written as *upwelling*.

(19) (B) nutricious.

The word *nutricious* in Option B is written incorrectly. This word should be written as *nutritious*.

(20) (A) whethering.

The words *whethering* and *weathering* are homophones. In this sentence, the word *whethering* is misspelled. *Whether* is a conjunction that is usually used to present a choice between a few possibilities, while *weather* in this context would mean that something is eroded or whittled down. Thus, *weathering* should be used in this sentence instead of *whethering*—which is not even a word.

(21) (B) There are many types of desert landscapes, such as erg, reg, hamada and desert pavement.

Of the four options presented, Option A is a run-on sentence with a comma splice. Option D is incorrect because a semicolon is used between an independent and a dependent sentence. Option C is missing one example of a desert landscape. Option B is the correct option as it joins both sentences together without any grammatical mistakes.

(22) (A) Semicolon.

A semicolon is used to connect two independent clauses that are related. Option B cannot be correct because the conjunction *and* cannot be used between these sentences due to the context. Option C cannot be correct because adding a comma between these sentences would make it a run-on sentence. In Option D, the conjunction *yet* cannot be used because this conjunction is used to join two ideas that are contrasting. Thus, Option A is the only correct one.

(23) (D) All of these landscapes were formed by wind erosion over thousands of years. Some of them even predate human civilization.

Option A is incorrect because it contains a determiner-noun disagreement; it is not grammatically correct. Since Kelsie wants to maintain her essay's tone and style, Option B cannot be chosen because it does not maintain the style of her other sentences. Option C has the same problem—it is very short and does not match the essay's style. Only Option D matches both the tone and style of the essay.

(24) (C) Yes, because the sentence is not relevant to the ideas presented in the previous sentences and is jarring to read.

This sentence does not add anything to the essay; it diverts the reader's attention by breaking the established rhythm. Thus, it should be removed from the paragraph.

(25) (C) III.

Options A, B and D cannot be used as argumentative introductions. Option A describes a similarity among civilizations. It cannot be used because argumentative essays do not discuss differences or similarities. Option B is simply a statement. Option D cannot work because it discusses an experience; it does not state an opinion or a point of view that can be defended.

Option C is most likely to be used as an introduction to an argumentative essay because it introduces the subject the writer is talking about, adds relevant and concise detail to make the subject seem interesting and contains a thesis statement at the end. This thesis statement gives the reader an idea about the position the writer will base his or her argument on.

(26) (A) I.

Compare-and-contrast essays discuss the similarities and differences between two things. Option B cannot be used because it is a statement and does not feature any contrasts. Option C could be used, but the second sentence does not add anything to the introduction as a whole and is irrelevant. Option D cannot work because it discusses an experience; it does not state an opinion or a point of view that can be defended.

Only Option A can be used to introduce a compare-and-contrast essay because it compares civilizations and describes a similarity among them.

(27) (D) V.

A speech is used to convince the audience or persuade them to believe in a certain point of view. Keeping this in mind, Options A, B and C cannot be used. Option A features a statement and is not persuasive at all. Option B is an example of an introduction that could be used in an argumentative essay and lacks a direct address to the audience. Option C starts with a sentence that talks about the difference between two things and devolves into something entirely different.

Option D uses first person and persuasive language. It begins by describing an experience in the writer's life in an attempt to convince the audience that a claim is legitimate. This option is highly likely to be found at the start of a speech.

(28) (A) Miscellaneous tasks.

A heading should give the reader some idea about what they are going to read about. A heading that does not match the content is misleading. Of all the options presented in this question, Option A seems to fit the context best, as the content under the heading describes very different jobs. Option B is similar to Option A, but it sounds too clunky and does not match the outline's formal tone; it is too colloquial and relaxed. Options C and D do not summarize the varied nature of the content's tasks under the heading.

(29) (C) Marketing.

Nona has listed some specific kinds of jobs under this particular subheading. All the jobs are connected to marketing, or are marketing jobs. The title presented in Option A is too specific and does not suit the content and subheadings. Similarly, the title listed in Option B is entirely unsuited to the content, as it does not match it at all. A title should always give a hint of the prose that would follow it. It should not be entirely different. Option C seems to work because all the jobs listed under the heading have one thing in common: marketing.

(30) (D) Real estate agents are salespeople, advisers, negotiators, researchers and managers: they are jacks of all trades.

Options A, B and C do not match Nona's specifications. She wants her introductory sentence(s) to give a brief overview of her whole essay. Option A does not work because it does not mention anything that would occur later in her essay. Option B could work, but the sentence ending in this option leaves something to be desired; it makes the sentence hard to understand. Option C cannot be used because it contains two sentences rather than one. This leaves Option D. It briefly states all the responsibilities of a real estate agent and meets all of Nona's requirements.

Essay Question: Sample Response

Describe the Most Vivid Experience of Your Life

It is a quiet spring morning, neither cold nor warm. The sun shines brightly from its perch in the sky like a lamp focused in one place. As I watch, a tiny, long-tailed bird with red plumage lands on a silvery branch of a poplar tree and chirps at me. I resist the urge to smile. Another bird lands beside it. Its feathers are a blend of orange and yellow. They strike up a tune as they fly around the verdant garden, crossing each other's paths in complicated patterns.

I sit on a wide, rough concrete ledge protruding from my house's wall and observe the swaying trees in my garden. It is some mysterious spring quality that deepens a plant's color from mere dull green to vivid shades of jade, lime, olive, chartreuse and viridian. It seems as if every leaf gains life in the spring season and shines with breathtaking inner vitality. Sunlight limns the droplets of dew on the leaves. They twinkle like diamonds. The wind, carrying the sweet scent of jasmine, caresses the leaves, causing their branches to sway. As a result, the dew on the leaves flies like crystal comets toward every part of the garden. A sharp coolness stings my cheek and drips down onto my clothes. A curious scent of ozone hangs in the air. The air feels charged.

As I watch, a fluffy tail emerges from the bushes around the poplar tree, and a squirrel pops out into view. It sees me and turns into a statue. We have a battle of stares, which the squirrel wins because I look away when I hear the sound of a twig snapping. When I look back, the squirrel stands up straight with a sniff and gives me a haughty look. I sigh and stand up. The furry blur vanishes into the bushes. I stretch and touch my toes. By the time I rise again, the wind has taken a sharp turn.

I hear the sound of a twig snapping again and whirl around just in time to see a snake land on the concrete ledge. It is as thick as a water pipe and covered in scales of mottled olive, yellow and light green. My muscles lock up. Fear drowns my emotions. I stare at it, horrified, my mind running in feverish circles, desperately trying to find a way out of this. The snake tilts its head and looks me over with an almost disdainful look. I clench my teeth to keep myself from shouting—my heart thuds. I can feel the blood pounding in my temples. The clouds break open, and rain washes over me. It is as if a giant has slanted a showerhead on top of the house. The rain pummels my hair and clothes until they are soaked.

Still, the snake watches. It has a large triangular head and a sinuous body. The snake slithers from side to side in graceful, almost hypnotizing, motions. Without warning, it rears up and slides off the ledge. For a moment, I can't help but stare at the snake, my body stock-still, my mind blank.

Before I can do anything, I am falling. I crash into the grass, dazed, and watch a tiny ladybug flare its wings and rush to hide behind a blade of grass. For a moment, my head is like a clear blue sky with no clouds in sight. Then the fear, shock and anxiety smash into me like a freight train. It feels like an hour has passed since I fell when I see my brother standing on the ledge, waving a sharp stick around in threatening motions. The snake sits on top of the twelve-foot-high boundary wall of the house and looks extremely put out. It looks at me as if to say, *What is wrong with you humans?*

I start laughing hysterically.

Test 3: Reading Questions

Carefully read the passages below and answer the questions at the end of each passage.

Passage 1: The history of homelessness in America. (For questions 1 through 5)

What are the causes of homelessness? Are there any effective strategies to help people exit homelessness? Homelessness is a major problem in America. There are more than 567,715 homeless people who sleep on the streets every night.

America experienced its first massive wave of homelessness after the Civil War. The major reason was the rise in the number of jobless veterans. They struggled to find permanent housing. Cities started to become more crowded over time. Millions of war prisoners who were freed from slavery struggled to find a place to live in the wake of the destructive war.

According to vagrancy laws imposed as a part of southern "black codes," the authorities had the right to arrest anyone who was unemployed. This shows the direct relationship between poverty, race and the criminalization of homelessness.

In the nineteenth century, skid rows provided shelter for most homeless men. Skid rows were not for women and children because various charitable religious organizations provided shelter for these segments of society. Skid rows were named after one of the streets in Seattle. This street was popular because logs were rolled down the road to be taken to the port. Skid rows provided shelter to more than 75,000 homeless men every night. The majority of these men were seasonal laborers belonging to agriculture, maritime, transportation, mining and more. They moved between cities in search of a living.

A chain of events that began in the 1950s and '60s changed what homelessness formerly meant to America. Skid rows and various other types of unsubsidized housing were demolished to renew cities. This included minority neighborhoods, which added to the homelessness America was already experiencing. In 1973, more than a million SROs were converted to suit other purposes or were demolished.

Homelessness is a combination of varied yet individual experiences caused by external and personal problems. Governments have not put forth much effort into finding a potential solution to this problem. People who experience homelessness believe that a housed person can never understand what it is like being homeless. They cannot relate to the experiences a homeless person has on the streets. The least housed people can do is to try to have sympathy for the homeless.

(1) What do you glean from this passage by skimming it?

(A) It explains what it is like being homeless in America.

(B) It shows what started the wave of homelessness in America.

(C) It explains which factors contributed to the rise in homelessness in America.

(D) All of the above.

(2) What does "vagrancy law" mean, as discussed in this passage?

(A) A law imposed to assure the continuance of white supremacy

(B) Laws designed to reinstate social control of slavery

(C) Laws removed by the Emancipation Proclamation and the Thirteenth Amendment to the Constitution

(D) All of the above

(3) When did America experience its first wave of homelessness?

(A) After the outbreak of the SARS virus

(B) After the Civil War, when millions of veterans lost their jobs

(C) After the assassination of the first US president

(D) None of the above

(4) What were skids rows named after?

(A) A famous street in Seattle

(B) A famous monument in Seattle

(C) A famous restaurant in Seattle

(D) A famous street in Chicago

(5) What factors cause a person to become homeless?

(A) Lack of education

(B) Bad family relationships

(C) A combination of varied yet individual experiences

(D) All of the above

Passage 2: Why are indie movies more interesting compared to mainstream Hollywood movies? (For questions 6 through 10)

There is one major reason Hollywood studios produce movies: to earn a profit. These studios are publicly traded corporations with many stakeholders. Therefore, they develop movies to appeal to the masses and make as much profit as they can.

The cinematic industry is losing its charm with time. There are several internet streaming services available where people can enjoy their desired content without leaving their homes. Hollywood studios are now backed into a corner. They cannot take big risks by exploring unusual topics. They must stick to the popular culture for a big win. They prefer brand-name blockbuster franchises over unique subject matters because already-established franchises have the highest likelihood of selling tickets at theaters. Moreover, it is easier to make a profit from these franchises by launching merchandise—for example, video games and toys.

This is one of the major reasons superhero movies are all the rage these days. Hollywood boardrooms are full of DC and Marvel fans. People are interested in watching these movies and purchasing merchandise and video games sold in their names. That is what provides movie makers with a great opportunity to profit from pop culture.

Independent movies are an entirely different genre of entertainment. An independent movie is made outside the studio system. Unlike studios, independent creators are not corporations in pursuit of profit. The majority of the time, they create movies to tell a story, express an idea or convey a vision. They create films simply because they want to. Their intent could be anything from making people laugh, cry, think or even cringe. It could be to gain recognition and further their careers. Or they might want to highlight a specific societal issue or promote inclusion and diversity. There are a plethora of reasons why indie filmmakers make movies. However, making money is not one of them.

It is wrong to state that mainstream movies created for mainstream moviegoers are not interesting. However, indie films are way more interesting compared to the majority of mainstream movie franchises. The reason is, independent moviemakers have more freedom to choose what they believe in. They think beyond earning the best return on their investments. Instead, they choose what suits their vision and the story they are trying to convey. This freedom leads to the creation of more dynamic and sincere movies.

(6) Why are major Hollywood movies produced?

(A) To please an audience

(B) To earn a profit

(C) To promote awareness about sensitive topics

(D) All of the above

(7) Why do Hollywood studios prefer brand-name blockbuster franchises over unique subject matters?

(A) Already-established franchises have the highest likelihood of selling tickets.

(B) It is easier to make a profit from these franchises by launching merchandise.

(C) These are publicly traded corporations with many stakeholders.

(D) All of the above.

(8) What is not a motive behind making an indie movie?

(A) Earning a profit

(B) Telling a story

(C) Exploring a complex subject matter

(D) Both B and C

(9) What do independent filmmakers prefer?

(A) Uniqueness over originality

(B) Gore over romance

(C) Authenticity over pop culture

(D) All of the above

(10) Independent movies are more_____than mainstream Hollywood movies.

Which of the following words best fits the blank?

(A) boring

(B) predictable

(C) dynamic

(D) None of the above

Passage 3: Why adequate sleep is important for steady weight loss. (For questions 11 through 15)

Losing weight is not easy. Most people struggle to lose weight, and even if you achieve your ideal body weight, it is not easy to maintain it. Those who are in the middle of their weight-loss journey often hear how getting enough sleep helps with weight loss. That is true! Even though scientists are trying to figure out the relationship between sleep and weight, many people claim to have lost excess weight just by fixing their sleep cycle. Apart from gaining excess weight, sleep deprivation affects your health in a variety of ways.

With the advent of technology, the life of an average American citizen has become busier. The amount of time spent sleeping has been significantly decreased. The quality of sleep has also been affected. Within the past few decades, an increase in Americans' body mass index has been observed. The trends show low-quality sleep has elevated the rates of obesity.

This drastic shift in trends has made scientists eager to study the potential relationship between sleep and weight. Various studies indicate inadequate sleep results in a variety of metabolic disorders. It leads to various chronic health conditions along with a higher risk of obesity and weight gain. There are various conflicts within the medical community about the nature of the relationship between the quality of sleep and weight loss. However, a connection exists between the two.

The intricate details about how sleep and weight are interconnected are yet to be explored. Various hypotheses lay the foundation for more research opportunities. This information will increase the understanding of the connection between weight and sleep. This research will also help in the development of more effective weight-loss methods.

One of the hypotheses regarding lack of sleep and weight gain is that lack of sleep increases your appetite. Scientists believe sleep affects your appetite. Appetite is much more than stomach grumbling. It is a phenomenon that is controlled by neurotransmitters. These are chemical messengers that trigger the communication between neurons, also referred to as nerve cells.

Two of the most important neurotransmitters involved with appetite include leptin and ghrelin. Leptin makes you feel fuller, whereas ghrelin makes you feel hungry. The levels of these neurotransmitters keep increasing and decreasing throughout the day. The changing levels of these neurotransmitters signal the body to consume calories.

When you do not get enough sleep, the regulation of neurotransmitters in your body is disturbed. According to a study, the level of ghrelin increased in men who got four hours of sleep. On the contrary, the level of leptin increased in those who enjoyed 10 hours of sleep.

When the level of ghrelin in your body is higher than the level of leptin, your appetite increases. You lose the feeling of fullness caused by leptin. Various studies have also revealed lack of sleep affects your preference of food. Sleep-deprived people tend to consume foods high in calories and carbohydrates.

(11) What do you make of this passage by skimming it?

(A) Getting enough sleep is important for losing weight.

(B) The more you sleep, the more you gain weight.

(C) Sleeping makes you obese.

(D) All of the above.

(12) What is causing the average American to gain weight?

(A) A lack of sleep

(B) A sedentary lifestyle

(C) A lack of physical activity

(D) All of the above

(13) What is the hypothesis regarding the connection between sleep and weight loss?

(A) There is a close connection between weight and sleep patterns.

(B) Sleeping less causes you to eat less.

(C) You need 12 hours of sleep to maintain an ideal weight.

(D) All of the above.

(14) Which hormones are involved in regulating appetite?

(A) Ghrelin and leptin

(B) Serotonin and cortisol

(C) Endorphins and insulin

(D) None of the above

(15) How do hormonal imbalances caused by a lack of sleep make you gain weight?

(A) Sleeplessness drops the level of leptin and increases the level of ghrelin.

(B) Sleeplessness boosts the level of leptin and drops the level of ghrelin.

(C) Sleeplessness increases the level of cortisol, which causes anxiety.

(D) Anxiety caused by the rise in the level of cortisol makes you eat more.

Passage 4: How are after-school activities important for keeping your child healthy and active? (For questions 16 through 20)

Your children's day is not over when the school bell rings. To make the rest of the day healthier and more productive, children should get involved in healthy after-school activities. The time children spend at school is often the most stressful. They have so much on their minds. Healthy after-school activities can relieve this stress by allowing children to spend some time away from books and the laptop screen. The after-school time can be filled with fun activities where children learn what interests them and enjoy their time while they are at it.

You can enroll children in a piano class, mixed martial arts academy, ballet classes and more. Remember to choose an activity that actually interests them. Studies have proved that after-school activities can make a big difference in a child's personal growth. Children become more disciplined and responsible. They develop better social skills and make new friends.

After-school activities make your children a lot happier and healthier. They get to learn new skills while enjoying time with children of the same age group. These activities ensure the safety of your children. You know exactly where they are after they head out.

After-school activities are scheduled. Parents are informed if their children do not attend or leave unaccounted for. Adults supervise these activities. This means your children will be monitored after school. These activities ensure that your children stay safe while indulging in an activity they enjoy. These activities also reduce the chances of your children skipping school.

After-school activities also make your children healthier and more active. These activities make children more productive in their general everyday life. Getting involved in some sort of physical activity daily is important for a healthy life. These activities ensure that your children make healthier choices when it comes to day-to-day life.

A healthy body means a healthy mind. It prevents depression and boosts self-esteem. By enrolling your children in an after-school program, you can rest assured that their mental health is good. By channeling energy into healthy activities, you can also prevent the development of criminal behavior in your child.

After-school activities can also prevent drug use because your children understand the importance of good health and know what is right for their body. The values they learn during these healthy activities stay with them in the years to come.

(16) What do you make of this passage after skimming it?

(A) After-school activities are important for growing children.

(B) After-school activities negatively impact a child's personality.

(C) After-school activities are a waste of time.

(D) All of the above.

(17) Children who partake in after-school activities are:

(A) Happier and healthier

(B) Stressed

(C) Anxious

(D) Hyperactive

(18) What are the benefits of after-school activities?

(A) They ensure your children's safety.

(B) They bring discipline to children's lives.

(C) They make children more active.

(D) All of the above.

(19) How do after-school activities impact the mental health of a child?

(A) They relieve stress caused by schoolwork.

(B) They help with homework.

(C) They make the child happier.

(D) All of the above.

(20) What do after-school activities help keep children away from?

(A) Criminal behavior

(B) Drugs use

(C) Both A and B

(D) None of the above

Passage 5: How to medicate your pet the right way. (For questions 21 through 25)

Giving your fur baby a pill can quickly turn into a disaster if your pet does not acquiesce to taking medicine as prescribed. To medicate your pet the right way, you need to ensure that you understand the instructions provided. Make sure you explain your pet's condition to the vet before asking for a prescription.

If you are confused about anything, ask your vet before starting to medicate your pet. Read the instructions carefully and follow them strictly. If your pet is already taking medicines, make sure you are aware of the consequences of combining certain medicines. Ask your vet whether you are supposed to medicate your pet on an empty or full stomach. Read and follow the instructions closely. Call your vet if you are confused about anything.

The best way to give your pet a pill is to hide the pill in your pet's favorite treats. When your pet is excited about eating its favorite food, it will swallow the pill along with the food. This will prevent your pet from biting into the medicine and tasting the bitter flavor.

Before you decide to mix medicines with pet food, consult your veterinarian. Certain foods interact with drugs and can be poisonous for your pet to consume. For example, never put tetracycline drugs into dairy products. The medication will bind to the food and will not be fully effective in treating your pet's condition.

Explore your pantry to look for food items to hide medication in. Use foods that your pet heartily enjoys and eats readily. One of the best options is peanut butter. You can cover the pill with a fragrant dab of sticky peanut butter. Scoop a spoonful and bring it to your pet's nose. Let it smell and lick it off.

You can roll the spoonful of peanut butter into a ball and hide the pill inside. Give it to your pet as a treat. However, before doing so, make sure that the peanut butter does not contain artificial sweeteners such as xylitol. These chemicals are toxic to dogs. Carefully read the ingredients before you choose a food item to hide the pill in.

Another great option is liverwurst. It is easy to roll this mushy meat product into a ball. You can create a pill pocket to hide the medicine in the center. Do not use your pet's canned food to hide the medication. Your pet could develop an aversion to the regular food if it bites into the pill and tastes the bitterness.

Cheese is another good option for hiding pills in. Go for low-sodium, part-skin, soft string or mozzarella cheese. It is low in calories, and the sodium level is optimum for your pet. You can easily slide pills and capsules into small cheese chunks without your pet even noticing. If that does not work, roll the slice of cheese into your hand and mold it around the pill.

(21) What do you make of this passage after skimming it?

(A) This passage explains the right way to medicate a pet.

(B) This passage tells how annoying it is to medicate a pet.

(C) This passage discusses why you should never give your pet medications.

(D) All of the above.

(22) What is the best approach for medicating your pet?

(A) Hide the pill in treats.

(B) Crush the pill and sprinkle it over food.

(C) Add artificial sweeteners to the pill.

(D) All of the above.

(23) In which type of food should you hide a pill?

(A) Pet treats

(B) Pet food

(C) Vegetables

(D) Fruits

(24) Which of the following options are ideal for hiding a pill?

(A) Peanut butter

(B) Cheese

(C) Liverwurst

(D) All of the above

(25) What should you keep in mind while hiding pills in your pet's food?

(A) Make sure the pill does not react with the ingredients in the food.

(B) Make sure the pill is completely dissolved with the food.

(C) Make sure the food does not taste bitter.

(D) None of the above.

Passage 6: Why should you meditate? (For questions 26 through 30)

The process of training your mind to focus is referred to as meditation. It is a technique for redirecting your thoughts. Meditation has been gaining a lot of traction in recent years. That is because people have started to discover that it offers health benefits they did not know of before. It is safe to say that meditation has now become a part of pop culture.

For most meditators, meditation is an ideal way to develop concentration and reduce stress. It is an ideal way to connect with yourself and become aware of your surroundings. This process helps people develop a variety of beneficial habits. It changes their perception of life. It makes them feel good. Various people have reported an uplift in their mood after a moderate meditation session. Meditation brings positive changes to your personality. You develop self-discipline and patience. It boosts your pain tolerance and improves your sleep patterns.

Stress relief is the first thought that comes to your mind when you hear the word *meditation*. It is one of the major motives behind meditation. Various studies have revealed that meditation is very effective and lives up to its reputation when it comes to stress reduction. It prevents the release of cortisol, a hormone that causes stress. It is also an ideal way to overcome stress-related health issues, including fibromyalgia, PSTD and irritable bowel syndrome.

By managing stress levels, meditation also helps with the reduction of anxiety. Less stress is equal to less anxiety. According to analysis, meditation is effective in reducing anxiety. The best results are observed in those who had the highest levels of anxiety.

This exercise is also ideal for those who want to improve their attention span. It boosts the endurance and strength of your attention. According to studies, listening to a meditation tape can enhance attention and accuracy while working on a project. It has also been revealed that people who meditate regularly perform a visual task better than those who do not. Meditators exhibit a better attention span than those who do not meditate. Meditation has the power to reverse patterns that lead to poor attention, worrying and distraction.

(26) What is the main idea of this passage?

(A) Meditation causes stress.

(B) Meditation relieves both physical and mental stress.

(C) Meditation is a part of Japanese culture.

(D) All of the above.

(27) How does meditation strengthen your mind?

(A) It improves focus and redirects your thoughts.

(B) It sharpens your mind.

(C) It relieves sleep apnea.

(D) None of the above.

(28) Meditation reduces the release of which hormone?

(A) Ghrelin

(B) Leptin

(C) Cortisol

(D) Insulin

(29) How does meditation help in reducing anxiety?

(A) Meditation leads to the management of stress, which in turn reduces anxiety.

(B) Meditation makes you sleepier.

(C) Both A and B.

(D) None of the above.

(30) How does meditation improve your attention?

(A) It lengthens your attention span.

(B) It improves your attention span.

(C) It improves your overall focus.

(D) All of the above.

Test 3: Math Questions

(1) If a scalene triangle has a side that is four centimeters long and another that is nine meters long, what is the perimeter and the area of the triangle in meters?

(A) 20 meters

(B) 16 meters

(C) 0.16 meters

(D) There isn't sufficient data to solve the problem.

(2) Tom was asked to take a mathematics test for his admission to a prestigious university. The test was 650 points, and he failed because he could attain only 43.5%. How many points out of 650 did he manage to score?

(A) 282.75

(B) 300

(C) 6.69

(D) 150

(3) Henry bought a wire that was originally in a square shape. One of its sides measured 400 centimeters. He wants to wrap that wire around a circular plate for decoration. What will be the radius of the circular wire in meters provided that the entire squared wire is used to decorate the plate?

(A) 4.00 meters

(B) 2.55 meters

(C) 5.09 meters

(D) 0.23 meters

(4) Emily wants to cover her small notebook with a plastic sheet to protect it from getting damaged. She wants to measure her notebook's length and width to determine the amount of plastic sheet she must have. Which of the following measuring instruments can help her best measure the length and width of her notebook?

(A) Stopwatch

(B) Measuring cylinder

(C) Meter ruler

(D) Scale

(5) There are 13 boys in a science class. The mean age of the 13 boys is 17.3 years. Provided that the boys' ages are 12, 14, 16, 20, 21, 14, 17, 18, 20, 20, x, 14 and 20 years, what is the value of x, the median, and the mode of the ages of the boys?

(A) x = 19 years; median = 18 years; mode = 20 years

(B) x = 17 years; median = 21 years; mode = 14 years

(C) x = 12 years; median = 20 years; mode = 19 years

(D) x = 13 years; median = 14 years; mode = 12 years

(6) On a well-maintained farm, 5/8 of the animals present are cows, and 2/3 of the remaining animals are goats. The farmer also has 20 hens. What is the total number of animals present on the farm?

(A) 200

(B) 160

(C) 20

(D) 350

(7) What is the value of x when $243^x \times 3 = 81 \div 1$?

(A) 3/5

(B) 5

(C) 0

(D) -1/5

(8) Anna buys 2,570 toys for her donation drives to different orphanages. On the first day, she donates 340 toys to one orphanage and 410 toys to another orphanage. On the third day, how much money in dollars is she left with to donate, provided that she bought each toy for 20 dollars?

(A) $15,000

(B) $36,400

(C) $18,000

(D) $23,450

(9) Emma buys two triangle cards. Both the triangle cards, A and B, have the same area. The base of triangle card A is 5 meters, and the height of triangle card A is 30 meters. If the base of triangle B is 15 meters, what is the height of triangle card B in centimeters?

(A) 1,000 centimeters

(B) 10 centimeters

(C) 5 centimeters

(D) 15 centimeters

(10) The data below represents the temperature measured at different times of a cold, breezy day in Houston over a period of five hours. Which of the following types of graphs is best to represent this data?

TIME	TEMPERATURE
1:00 a.m.	10 degrees Celsius
2:00 a.m.	5 degrees Celsius
3:00 a.m.	12 degrees Celsius
4:00 a.m.	13 degrees Celsius
5:00 a.m.	7 degrees Celsius

(A) Pie chart

(B) Line graph

(C) Picture graph

(D) Area chart

(11) Miss Sasha asked her students to convert 70 micrometers and 1,000 nanometers into the SI base unit for length. Which of the following units should the students convert the lengths to?

(A) Centimeters

(B) Millimeters

(C) Meters

(D) Pico meters

(12) A computer science test was to be held at 11:01 a.m. However, due to a power breakdown, the test got delayed by 33 minutes. If the test duration was 1 hour 25 minutes and there was no further delay, at what time did the rescheduled test end?

(A) 12:59 a.m.

(B) 12:59 p.m.

(C) 12:25 p.m.

(C) 10:59 a.m.

(13) When Sam solved the equation $y = 19 - (12 \times 3^2 + 14)$, he got the answer -257. However, the answer he obtained was wrong. Which of the following is the correct value for y?

(A) -103

(B) 103

(C) 257

(D) 12

(14) Which of the following represents 5^{12} the best?

(A) 5 x 12

(B) 5^{10} x 25

(C) 5 x 5 x 5 x 5 x 5 x 5 x 125

(D) $10^{24}/2$

(15) If the area of a trapezoid is 500 cm² and the sum of its parallel sides is 250 centimeters, what is the height of the trapezoid in meters?

(A) 2 meters

(B) 10 meters

(C) 0.04 meters

(D) 0.07 meters

(16) The mean mass of a group of 12 female athletes is 55 kg. Two female athletes of masses 36 kg and 45 kg left the group. What is the new mean mass of the group of athletes in grams after the two athletes left?

(A) 57,900 grams

(B) 48,250 grams

(C) 12,345 grams

(D) 34,901 grams

(17) Georgina buys 160 bottles of juice for a birthday party she has organized at her place. The total number of guests invited is 195. She figures out that for every three guests, she needs to keep two bottles of juice aside. Which of the following fractions is also representative of the same information?

(A) 178/267

(B) 1/6

(C) 312/624

(D) 1,234/5,678

(18) In a mathematics class of 700 students, 230 students are boys, and the remaining students are girls. What percentage of students in the class are girls?

(A) 67%

(B) 12%

(C) 33%

(D) 45%

(19) The heights of 17 students in a class are 120, 75, 80, 63, 65, 71, 111, 121, 100, 75, 119, 68, 75, 57, 89, 101 and 90 cm. What are the mode and the median height of the 17 students?

(A) Mode = 111 cm; median = 121 cm

(B) Mode = 75 cm; median = 80 cm

(C) Mode = 121 cm; median = 75 cm

(D) Mode = 111 cm; median = 143 cm

(20) What is the value of z when $z = 21 + (2 \times 12^2 - 25)$?

(A) 238

(B) 284

(C) 259

(D) 121

(21) If one angle of an equilateral triangle is 60 degrees, what are the values of the other two angles?

(A) There is not sufficient data to solve this problem

(B) 120 degrees

(C) 60 degrees

(D) 45 degrees

(22) When the perimeter of a circular field is 150 centimeters, what is the area of half of the same circular field in meters?

(A) 0.179 m²

(B) 0.0895 m²

(C) 1.234 m²

(D) 4.567 m²

(23) What is the value of y when $(1/2^{-1}) \div (1/16^y) = 2^6 \times 8$?

(A) y = 2

(B) y = -2

(C) y = 3

(D) y = 1

(24) A couple orders 50 boxes of sweets to distribute among their relatives and friends. They distribute five boxes to their friends and 21 boxes to their close family members. If the mass of each box of sweets is two kilograms, what is the total mass in grams of the boxes of sweets they could not distribute?

(A) 48,000 grams

(B) 52 grams

(C) 123 grams

(D) 670 grams

(25) The following table represents the scores Tim obtained in different subjects. If a student scores 50% or below, they are considered failing. However, if they score above 50% and below 60%, they receive a B. Similarly, if they score 60% or below 70%, they receive an A, whereas scoring 70% or above results in an A*. What grade did Tim get?

Subject	Scores out of 100
Physics	75
Computer Science	50
Mathematics	81
Chemistry	93

(A) A

(B) Fail

(C) A*

(D) B

(26) If two days are equal to 172,800 seconds, how many seconds make up six and a half days?

(A) 561,600 seconds

(B) 9,360 seconds

(C) 123,400 seconds

(D) 56,742 seconds

(27) Sarah wanted to cook chicken soup for 500 people coming over to her home. She required 3 kg of chicken. However, she had more chicken than required. Therefore, she separated some of it and wanted to see if she had separated out 3 kg. Which of the measuring instruments can she use to verify her estimation?

(A) Measuring cylinder

(B) Scale

(C) Inch tape measure

(D) Meter ruler

(28) The width of a rectangle is one-fourth of its length. If the perimeter of the rectangle is 200 centimeters, what are the length and the width of the rectangle in meters?

(A) Length = 80 m; width = 20 m

(B) Length = 40 m; width = 80 m

(C) Length = 0.08 m; width = 0.2 m

(D) Length = 0.04 m; width = 0.04 m

(29) If 5^0 is equal to 1 and 135^0 is also equal to 1, what is the value of $3,456^0$?

(A) 0

(B) 17,325

(C) 1

(D) 2

(30) Which of the following fractions represents 35.6% the best?

(A) 89/250

(B) 1/5

(C) 134/245

(D) 54/124

Test 3: Writing Questions

For questions 1 through 3: The following sentences were written by four students as the introductory sentences of a few different types of essays.

I. Raising taxes without any reason is appalling and wrong because sudden taxes can reduce business revenue and can, at times, bankrupt others, so we should try to keep taxes down.

II. One main difference between the Allies and the Axis in World War II was that the Allied powers had an enormous economic and industrial capacity in contrast to the economies and industries of the Axis countries, which had been badly damaged by World War I.

III. When Alfred Wegener, in 1912, proposed the idea of continental drift, his theory was not met with widespread support; however, half a century later, using better technology and research methods to observe the movement of continents, geologists proved his theory was correct.

IV. Climate change is a devastating phenomenon. If left to flourish without supervision, it will damage the earth beyond its capacity to recover.

(1) Which of the following sentences is most likely to be used in a compare-and-contrast essay?

(A) I

(B) II

(C) III

(D) IV

(2) Which of the following sentences is most likely to be used as a thesis statement in an argumentative essay (an essay written to convince a reader that a certain point of view is correct)?

(A) I

(B) II

(C) III

(D) IV

(3) Which of the following sentences is most likely to be used as an introductory statement in a persuasive essay?

(A) I

(B) II

(C) III

(D) IV

(4) A student named Catherine wrote the paragraph below for an assignment at school.

"(1) A house crouched on the four-thousand-square foot lot like a tiger hunkering over its kill. (2) Tall redwood trees back the house, covered in red moss. (3) Kudzu sheaths three huge boulders that sat to the right of the house."

What kind of error can be found in the paragraph above?

(A) Incorrect capitalization

(B) Run-on sentences

(C) Verb-tense errors

(D) Subject-verb disagreement

(5) Which word is not spelled correctly?

(A) Hellinistic

(B) Aborigine

(C) Finagle

(D) Piteous

(6) Calvin is writing the conclusion of his manuscript. He pens the last word and settles back, exhausted. He has been averaging 2,000 words per day for the past two months.

What is the next step in the writing process?

(A) Drafting

(B) Publishing

(C) Editing

(D) Revising

(7) A high school student wrote a large part of her narrative essay in the passive voice. The teacher told the student to revise the work. What is the best active voice translation for the sentence below from the narrative essay?

"The expensive watch and the stunning diamond ring were designed by the renowned jeweler."

(A) The expensive watch was designed by the renowned jeweler, who also designed the stunning diamond ring.

(B) The renowned jeweler designed the expensive watch and the stunning diamond ring.

(C) The diamond ring was designed by the renowned jeweler, who made an expensive watch.

(D) The jeweler designed the stunning diamond ring and the expensive watch.

(8) The Bayley Tower was sheathed in blue glass that darkened as the building gained height and rose into the sky like the spear of a mighty giant from an ancient legend.

What is the subject of the sentence above?

(A) Sheathed

(B) Ancient

(C) Blue glass

(D) The Bayley Tower

(9) Sienna Hawke is writing an essay for her ancient history class. She wants to write an essay that compares the Greek and Roman cultures. She wants her essay to be informative, logical and accurate.

What kind of reference material should she use?

(A) An encyclopedia

(B) An article about Greek culture

(C) Books on Roman and Greek culture

(D) Abstracts

(10) Shelly was invited to dinner by a friend whose mother was renowned for her pies; when she took her first bite, she knew that all the claims were true because it was the best pie she had ever tasted in her life.

What is the simple predicate in the sentence above?

(A) Invited

(B) Renowned

(C) Took

(D) Knew

(11) The tree stand motionless, as tall as a hundred men stacked upright, with a deep maroon trunk that was glistening with red sap and enormous black leaves that shadowed the area around it for leagues.

What errors can be found in the sentence above?

(A) Subject-verb error

(B) Incorrect comma usage

(C) Incorrect word usage

(D) Verb-tense errors

For questions 12 through 17: In the sentences below, four words are underlined and have letters underneath them. Read each sentence and choose the underlined portion that contains a grammatical, capitalization, word-use, spelling or punctuation error. **None of the sentences has more than one error.**

(12) The attack on Pearl Harbor was meant to <u>destroy</u> the US <u>pacific fleet</u> to
                                             A   B

keep it from <u>interfering</u> in planned Japanese military actions against the United
               C

Kingdom, France, and the <u>United States</u> in Central and Southeast Asia.
                            D

(13) Iridium, <u>the second-densest</u> element known to man after osmium, <u>was</u> a very hard,
               A   B

silver-white, brittle, very rare, and highly <u>corrosion</u>-resistant metal with a high melting
                                     C

point<u>;</u> it is mostly used as a hardening agent for platinum, but it can also be used to tip
    D

pens and compass bearings.

(14) Making a single statement about the causes of soil <u>degradation</u>, without
                                              A

disregarding the complexity of such an <u>occurence,</u> is challenging because the soil
                                    B

degradation can be caused by water erosion, wind erosion, <u>acidification</u>, eutrophication,
                                                          C

atmospheric deposition, climate change and <u>salinization</u> of the soil.
                                                   D

(15) When the tensions between the United States of America and the <u>confederate</u>
                                                                      A
<u>states</u> of America finally erupted, the first shots were fired at Fort Sumter in South
                                      B
Carolina, <u>and</u> the American Civil War <u>broke</u> out.
          C   D

(16) About 6,000 years ago, Northern Africa—one of the most arid regions on <u>Earth and</u>
                                            A   B
home to the <u>largest</u> desert in the world—used to be a humid tropical area that once
            C
flourished with <u>grenery</u>.
                D

(17) The main difference between a <u>democracy</u> and a republic is that in a republic,

people
                                            A
have rights that cannot be voted away by a majority vote because these rights are <u>routed</u>
                                                                                   B
in law: whereas, in a democracy, the individual or any group of individuals in a minority
      C   D
have no protection against the power of the majority.

(18) In which of the following sentences is a comma not used correctly?

(A) The Roman Empire reigned over the city of Rome for over 2,000 years until its
eventual demise.

(B) "Sure, I have twenty minutes to burn until I have to go pick up the kids from school,"
said Deanna.

(C) Alan Kinston and Georgina Kincaid are successful investment bankers who take
great pride in their achievements.

(D) Orographic or relief rainfall happens when air is forced to rise over a mountain or
any barrier, and is forced to cool down, condense and form rain.

(19) The depths of the Challenger Deep were <u>disturbed</u> for the first time by humans Jacques Piccard and Don Walsh in the 1960s.

Which part of speech is underlined in the sentence above?

(A) A quantifier

(B) An adverb

(C) A verb

(D) An adjective

For questions 20 through 23: The following short essay was written by Dylan for a school assignment.

Desert Types: Hot and Cold.

By Dylan Hern

(1) A desert is classified as a sparsely vegetated, arid region where rainfall is sporadic or very low. (2) There are two types of deserts in the world. (3) They are hot and cold. (4) Cold deserts, such as the Arctic and the Antarctic desert, are found on the poles of the earth, while hot deserts, such as the Sahara or the Gobi, are found in warm parts of the world.

(5) However, both these deserts are different. (6) Antarctica, located in the southern hemisphere, is a desert because of its low amount of precipitation and snow events. (7) When it does snow, the snow piles up onto the existing snow and builds up over time into ice sheets. (8) The Sahara Desert, on the other hand, is classified as a desert because of its aridity, the sparseness of vegetation and its low annual precipitation events. (9) Ranging from zero to about four inches of rain every year.

(20) Dylan wants to join sentences 2 and 3 to create a clear, concise, logical and grammatically correct sentence. Which choice most effectively combines sentences 1 and 2?

(A) There are two types of deserts in the world, they are hot and cold.

(B) There are two types of deserts in the world: hot and cold.

(C) There are two types of deserts in the world; hot and cold.

(D) Cold and hot; are the two types of deserts in the world.

(21) As Dylan revises his work, he realizes that he should connect sentences 8 and 9 because sentence 9 continues the ideas mentioned in sentence 8.

"(8) The Sahara Desert, on the other hand, is classified as a desert because of its aridity, the sparseness of vegetation, and its low annual precipitation events. (9) Ranging from zero to about four inches of rain every year."

What transition word, conjunction or punctuation mark should he choose to connect these two sentences?

(A) Semicolon

(B) And

(C) That

(D) Comma

(22) Dylan is considering adding some facts to his essay. He wants to add some facts to sentence 6 to support his claim about Antarctica being a desert.

"Antarctica, located in the southern hemisphere, is a desert because of its low amount of precipitation and snow events."

Which choice provides the best supporting details for the claim made in the sentence?

(A) Precipitation is scarce, so the whole Sahara Desert receives around 3.9 inches of rain every year.

(B) It is extremely dry, averaging around 6.5 inches of precipitation every year.

(C) In 1983, at Vostok Station, the lowest temperature ever recorded in Antarctica was 89° Celsius.

(D) The climate in the desert ranges from hot summers to cool winters.

(23) Dylan is considering removing the following sentence to tighten the essay and remove extra words: "However, both these deserts are different."

Should Dylan delete this sentence?

(A) Yes, because the sentence differs from the tone Dylan created through his writing style in the paragraph.

(B) No, because the sentence connects the ideas mentioned in the preceding paragraph to the ideas mentioned in the next paragraph.

(C) Yes, because the sentence repeats information that is already mentioned elsewhere in the essay.

(D) No, because the sentence helps develop the main topic of the essay and adds more information to the essay as a whole.

(24) In which of the following sentences is a comma not used correctly?

(A) The hunter skirted the swampy soil, went around the mound of dried leaves, bypassed the horde of critters that tried to climb up his legs and reached the bridge.

(B) The first time she saw a baby macaw, she was mesmerized: it had a small, hard beak; colorful red green and blue dappled feathers; and little tiny feet.

(C) All of his children were in college. Alyssa was studying engineering; Alex was completing his master's in computer science; and Celina was learning how to become a cardiologist.

(D) She went into her room, stepped around the clothes on the floor and flopped onto her bed.

(25) It was high noon—the sun was at its zenith—when a man walked out of the building, his stride graceful as he glides down the stairs, his steps as light as feathers and almost as soundless.

What error can be found in the sentence above?

(A) Incorrect comma usage

(B) Incorrect word usage

(C) Incorrect capitalization

(D) Verb-tense errors

(26) Which word is not spelled correctly?

(A) Luminesced

(B) Crumpled

(C) Siphon

(D) Pinacle

(27) Kevin finished the final draft of his thesis the day before yesterday. Using Track Changes in Microsoft Word, he is now removing any typos, correcting any spelling and capitalization errors, checking sentences for tense changes and checking the prose for clarity.

Which step of the writing process is Kevin currently at?

(A) Proofreading

(B) Editing

(C) Revising

(D) Drafting

(28) Gilliam is writing a paper about the famous Italian philosopher and writer Niccolò Machiavelli. She wants to find out his personal history, his birthplace, the year he was born and the reason why the literature he wrote became so famous.

What kind of reference material should she use?

A) An encyclopedia

B) A biography of Niccolò Machiavelli

C) An article about Machiavelli, his life and his influence

D) An atlas

(29) "Though he reined for several years over the people of the Marshall Kingdom, he never had his fill."

What error can be found in the sentence above?

(A) Incorrect comma usage

(B) Verb-tense errors

(C) Subject-verb disagreement

(D) Incorrect word usage

(30) Which word is not spelled correctly?

(A) Didactic

(B) Solisits

(C) Apprehension

(D) Desert

Essay Question: Every year, countless high school and college students are caught and expelled based on cheating. Many suffer severe consequences due to one misdemeanor.

If caught, should cheaters be given another chance?

Test 3: Reading Answers & Explanations

(1) (D) All of the above.

Skimming is a prereading activity in which the reader skims a piece of text to get a general overview of the content before reading. This activity gives a vague idea of what to expect from a passage. By skimming this passage, we learn what it is like being homeless in America. The passage reveals what started the wave of homelessness in America. It also explains which factors contributed to the rise in homelessness in the United States.

(2) (D) All of the above.

Before reading a passage in detail, readers should identify the words or phrases they do not understand. Most readers will not be familiar with the term *vagrancy laws*. Therefore, it is ideal to look it up before they start reading the passage in detail.

Vagrancy law was imposed to assure the continuance of white supremacy. It was designed to reinstate the social control of slavery. This law had been removed by the Emancipation Proclamation and the Thirteenth Amendment to the Constitution.

(3) (B) After the Civil War, when millions of veterans lost their jobs.

According to this passage, America went through its first wave of homelessness after the Civil War. After this war, millions of veterans lost their jobs and homes.

(4) (A) A famous street in Seattle.

Skid rows were shelters where homeless men used to sleep at night. They were named after a famous street in Seattle.

(5) (C) A combination of varied yet individual experiences.

The majority of the time, the factors that lead to homelessness are a combination of varied yet individual experiences. These experiences are the results of both external and internal problems.

(6) (B) To earn a profit.

Per the passage, the main motive behind the production of a mainstream Hollywood movie is to earn a profit. These movies have various stakeholders involved. Therefore, the filmmakers' first motive is to try to make as much money as they can in order to pay back the investors in the project.

(7) (D) All of the above.

There are various reasons why Hollywood studios prefer brand-name blockbuster franchises over unique subject matters. They are publicly traded corporations with many stakeholders. Therefore, they need to make money before anything else. It is also because already-established franchises have the highest likelihood of selling tickets. Moreover, it is easier to make a profit from these franchises by launching merchandise.

(8) (A) Earning a profit.

Earning a profit is the last motive of indie filmmakers. They aim to tell a story or convey an idea. Indie movies are also produced to highlight complex subject matters.

(9) (C) Authenticity over pop culture.

In the majority of cases, what pleases the audience does not matter to indie filmmakers. They always choose authenticity over pop culture. They show what they believe in rather than what makes them more money.

(10) (C) dynamic.

When we compare mainstream cinema with independent movies, we find that the majority of mainstream Hollywood movies are predictable, formulaic and monotonous. On the contrary, independent movies are rather dynamic when compared to Hollywood movies.

(11) (A) Getting enough sleep is important for losing weight.

Skimming is when the reader goes over content without getting into the details. This prereading activity provides an overview of what the passage is going to be about. By skimming this passage, the reader learns how getting enough sleep is important for losing weight.

(12) (D) All of the above.

The average American today is more obese than people were a decade ago. There are various factors behind that. Some of them include lack of proper sleep, a sedentary lifestyle and a lack of physical activity.

(13) (A) There is a close connection between weight and your sleep pattern.

There is a common hypothesis regarding the connection between sleep and weight loss, according to which your body weight and sleep patterns are interrelated. The sounder sleep you enjoy, the less weight you will gain.

(14) (A) Ghrelin and leptin.

There are two neurotransmitters involved when it comes to regulating appetite in the human body. Ghrelin is the hormone that signals the body that it is time to consume some calories. On the other hand, leptin is the hormone that creates the sense of fullness that prevents overeating.

(15) (A) Sleeplessness drops the level of leptin and increases the level of ghrelin.

Sleeplessness imbalances the hormones involved with your appetite. It drops the level of leptin level and increases the level of ghrelin, which causes you to feel hungry more frequently.

(16) (A) After-school activities are important for growing children.

This passage lists the benefits of after-school activities for young children. The writer wants to persuade parents to enroll their children in after-school programs to improve their well-being.

(17) (A) Happier and healthier.

Per the passage, children who partake in after-school activities are often healthier and happier than those who only attend school.

(18) (D) All of the above.

There are various benefits to enrolling your children in after-school programs. Some of them include ensuring your children's safety, adding more discipline to their lives and making them more active.

(19) (A) They relieve stress caused by schoolwork.

After-school activities allow children to take a break from studies to indulge in healthy physical activities that keep them active. They get to learn important life lessons while enjoying their time with children of their own age.

(20) (C) Both A and B.

After-school activities provide children with a place to go after school. If left unsupervised, children may get into dangerous activities. After-school activities help keep children from developing criminal behavior. They may also prevent them from using drugs.

(21) (A) This passage explains the right way to medicate a pet.

In this passage, the writer explains the best way to medicate your pet.

(22) (A) Hide the pill in treats.

According to this passage, the best way to medicate your pet is to hide pills in treats.

(23) (A) Pet treats.

According to the author, you should never hide a pill in regular pet food because your cat or dog will develop an aversion to its regular food if it associates the bitter pill with the food. It is better to hide the pill in treats your pet is excited to have.

(24) (D) All of the above.

The best treats for hiding a pill to medicate your pet include peanut butter, liverwurst and cheese.

(25) (A) Make sure the pill does not react with the ingredients in the food.

While hiding a pill in your pet's treats, make sure the medication's ingredients do not react with the ingredients of the food.

(26) (B) Meditation relieves both physical and mental stress.

Meditation is the ideal exercise for those who suffer from physical and mental stress.

(27) (A) It improves focus and redirects your thoughts.

Meditation is the perfect exercise to improve your focus and redirect your thoughts.

(28) (C) Cortisol.

Meditation reduces the release of cortisol hormone, which in turn relieves stress and anxiety.

(29) (A) Meditation leads to the management of stress, which in turn reduces anxiety.

Meditation reduces stress. As a result, it reduces the release of cortisol, which reduces anxiety.

(30) (D) All of the above.

Meditation maximizes your attention span and focus.

Test 3: Math Answers & Explanations

(1) (D) There isn't sufficient data to solve the problem.

The perimeter of a triangle is the sum of all of its three sides. In a scalene triangle, each side is a different length. But the lengths of only two sides are provided in the question.

To calculate the area, the base and the height need to be known. However, in the question, the value for the height is not given.

(2) (A) 282.75.

The formula for calculating percentage:

Percentage attained = (points obtained/total points) x 100

Let the points obtained be x.

43.5% = x/650 x 100

Remove the percentage sign by dividing 43.5% by 100.

43.5/100 = x/650

Multiply 650 with 43.5/100 to obtain the value of x.

x = 282.75 points.

(3) (B) 2.55 meters.

Since the answer is required in meters, convert the units.

1 cm = 1/100 m

Therefore, 400 cm = 400/100 = 4 m.

The square wire's perimeter is equal to the perimeter (circumference) of the circular wire because the entire length of the square wire is used when the shape is changed.

Perimeter of square = 4 (length).

Perimeter of square = 4 x 4 = 16 meters

Perimeter/circumference of circle = $2\pi r$

$16 = 2\pi r$

Divide 16 by 2π and obtain the value of r.

$16/2\pi = r = 2.55$ meters.

(4) (C) Meter ruler.

A stopwatch is used to measure time; a measuring cylinder is used to measure the volume of a liquid and a scale measures the mass of an object. A meter ruler is used to measure lengths.

(5) (A) x = 19 years; median = 18 years; mode = 20 years.

Mean is the average value of the data.

The formula for calculating mean is:

Mean = sum of data/total number of data

The sum of data (ages) is 12 + 14 + 16 + 20 + 21 + 14 + 17 + 18 + 20 + 20+ 14 + 20 + x

Substitute the value of the mean, total number of data and the sum of data in the formula to obtain the value of x.

$17.3 = 206 + x/13$

Multiply 17.3 with 13 to obtain 224.9.

$224.9 = 206 + x$

Subtract 224.9 − 206 to obtain the value of x.

x = 18.9, which is approximately equal to 19 years.

Mode is the most frequently occurring value in the data. In this set of values, 20 years is the most frequently occurring value and is repeated four times. Hence, the mode age is 20 years.

Median is the middle value of the data. To find the median, first arrange the set of values in ascending order.

12, 14, 14, 14, 16, 17, 18, 19, 20, 20, 20, 20, 21 is the new order of data.

To find the median, the formula is n + 1/2, where n is the total number of data.

13 + 1 / 2 = seventh position

The value at the seventh position is 18 years. Hence, the median age is 18 years.

(6) (B) 160.

Let the total number of animals be x.

The number of cows = (5/8) (x)

To find the remaining number of animals, subtract the number of cows from the total number of animals.

Remaining animals except cows = x − (5/8) (x)

To find the number of goats, multiply 2/3 with the expression for the remaining animals.

The number of goats = 2/3 (x − (5/8) (x)) = 1/4 (x)

Add the number of hens and the two expressions for cows and goats. Equate the sum with x, which is the total number of animals.

20 + (5/8) (x) + (1/4) (x) = x

Add 5x/8 and x/4 to obtain 7x/8.

20 + (7/8) (x) = x

Subtract (7/8) (x) from x.

20 = x − (7/8) (x)

20 = (1/8) (x)

Multiply 8 with 20 to obtain the value of x.

20 x 8 = x = 160 animals on the farm.

(7) (A) 3/5.

243^x can also be written as 3^{5x}.

3 can also be written as 3^1 because if a number does not have any power, the power is actually 1.

81 can be written as 3 x 3 x 3 x 3 and 3 x 3 x 3 x 3 can also be written 3^4.

1 can also be written as 3^0 because any number with zero as its power is equal to 1.

Hence, the equation can be written as $3^{5x} \times 3^1 = 3^4 \div 3^0$.

Taking the left-hand side, when the bases of the terms are the same and the terms are multiplying, their powers add up.

Taking the right-hand side, when the bases of the terms are the same and the terms are divided, their powers get subtracted from each other.

$3^{5x} + 1 = 3^{4-0}$

If the terms on both sides of the = sign have the same base, their powers are also equal.

5x + 1 = 4

Subtract 1 from 4 and divide it by 5 to obtain the value of x.

x = 3/5.

(8) (B) $36,400.

To find the cost of remaining toys, first find the number of toys. To find the number of toys Anna is left with at the end, subtract 340 and 410 from 2,570.

2,570 − 340 − 410 = 1,820 toys

When 1 toy costs $20, the cost of 1,820 toys will be:

1,820 x 20 = $36,400.

(9) (A) 1,000 centimeters.

Since the answer is required in centimeters, convert the units.

1 meter = 100 centimeters

Therefore:

5 meters = 5 x 100 = 500 centimeters

30 meters = 30 x 100 = 3,000 centimeters

15 meters = 15 x 100 = 1,500 centimeters

The base of triangle A is 500 centimeters and the height of triangle A is 3,000 centimeters.

The base of triangle B is 1,500 centimeters.

The area of triangle A = 1/2 x base x height.

Substitute the values of base and height to obtain the area of triangle A.

Area of triangle A = 500 x 3,000

Area of triangle A = 750,000 cm²

The area of triangle A is equal to the area of triangle B.

Area of triangle B = 1/2 x base x height.

Substitute the values of area and base to obtain the value of the height of triangle B.

750,000 = 1/2 x 1,500 x height

Multiply 2 with 750,000 and divide it with 1,500 to obtain the value of height.

Height of triangular card B = 750,000 x 2 / 1,500 = 1,000 centimeters.

(10) (B) Line graph.

Line graphs are used to represent changes over a short period. For this data, a line graph will be used because changes in Houston's temperature are recorded over a period of five hours from 1:00 a.m. to 5:00 a.m.

(11) (C) Meters.

The SI base units are the standardized units set by the International System of Units for the seven base quantities from which other quantities are derived. These seven quantities include the length of an object. Although lengths can be measured in different units, such as centimeters, millimeters, micrometers, etc., the SI base unit for length is meters.

(12) (B) 12:59 p.m.

If the test was to start at 11:01 a.m. but got delayed by 33 minutes, it started at 11:34 a.m. Add 33 minutes to 01 to obtain 34.

The duration of the test was 1 hour and 25 minutes.

If one hour is added to 11:34, it becomes 12:34. However, after the clock strikes 12, a.m. changes into p.m. It will thus be 12:34 p.m.

When 25 minutes are added to 12:34 p.m., the time changes to 12:59 p.m. The test, therefore, ended at 12:59 p.m.

(13) (A) -103.

Apply PEMDAS.

First, solve the parentheses.

$3^2 = 9$. Multiply 9 by 12 and obtain 108.

$y = 19 - (108 + 14)$

Add 14 to 108 to obtain 122.

$y = 19 - 122$

Subtract 122 from 19 to obtain the correct value for y.

y = -103

Sam obtained -257 because he followed the following wrong order of operations.

He took the square of 3 and added 14 to it.

y = 19 - (12 x 23)

He then multiplied 12 by 23 to obtain 276.

y = 19 – 276

He then subtracted -276 from 19 to obtain the wrong value of y, which is -257.

(14) (B) 5^{10} x 25.

25 can also be written as 5^2.

5^{10} x 5^2

If the bases of the terms are the same and the terms are multiplied, their powers add up.

$5^{10 + 2} = 5^{12}$

Taking each option:

5 x 12 = 60

5 X 5 X 5 X 5 X 5 X 5 X 125 = 5 X 5 X 5 X 5 X 5 X 5 X 5 X 5 X 5 = 5^9

10^{24}/2 = 5 x 10^{23}

None of these answers is equal to 5^{12} except Option B.

(15) (C) 0.04 meters.

The formula for the area of a trapezoid is:

Area of trapezoid = 1/2 x height x (sum of parallel sides)

Substitute the values of the area and the sum of parallel sides in the formula.

500 = 1/2 x height x (250)

Multiply 2 by 500 and divide it by 250 to obtain the value of height.

(500 x 2)/250 = height = 4 centimeters

Since the answer is required in meters, convert the units of the height.

1 cm = 1/100 meters

Hence, 4 centimeters = 4/100 = 0.04 meters.

(16) (A) 57,900 grams.

Mean is the average value of the data.

The formula for calculating mean is:

Mean = sum of data/total number of data

Substitute the values of mean and the total number of data to obtain the athletes' total masses.

55 = sum of masses/12

Multiply 12 by 55 to obtain 660 as the sum of masses.

Subtract 36 and 45 from 660 to obtain the new sum of masses after the two athletes left the group. The total number of athletes in the group is now 12 − 2 = 10.

660 − 36 − 45 = 579

Calculate the new mean by putting the information in the formula.

Mean = 579/10

Mean = 57.9 kg

Since the answer is required in grams, convert the units of the mean.

1 kg = 1,000 grams

Hence, 57.9 kg = 57,900 grams.

(17) (A) 178/267.

Taking each option:

1/6 is already in its most simplified form.

312/624 is further divisible by 312. 312 divided by 312 is equal to 1, and 624 divided by 312 is equal to 2. The simplified form of 312/624 is 1/2.

1,234/5,678 is further divisible by 2. 1,234 divided by 2 is equal to 617, and 5,678 divided by 2 is equal to 2,839. The simplified form of 1,234/5,678 is 617/2,839.

However, 178/267 gives 2/3 because both 178 and 267 are further divisible by 89. 178 divided by 89 is equal to 2, and 267 divided by 89 is equal to 3.

(18) (A) 67%.

To calculate the number of girls in the class, subtract the number of boys from the total number of students in the class.

Number of girls = 700 − 230 = 470

To calculate the percentage, the formula is:

Percentage of girls = (number of girls/total students) x 100

Percentage of girls = (470/700) x 100

Percentage of girls = 67%.

(19) (B) Mode = 75 cm; median = 80 cm.

Mode is the most frequently occurring value in the data. In this set of values, 75 cm is repeated three times and more than any other height. Hence, the mode of this data is 75 cm.

Median is the middle value of the data. To find the median, first arrange the data in ascending order.

57, 63, 65, 68, 71, 75, 75, 75, 80, 89, 90, 100, 101, 111, 119, 120, 121 is the new order of data.

The median position can be found out by the formula $(n + 1)/2$, where n is the total number of data.

$(n + 1)/2 = (17 + 1)/2 =$ ninth position

In the ninth position, the height is 80 cm, and hence the median is 80 cm.

(20) (B) 284.

Apply PEMDAS to solve $z = 21 + (2 \times 12^2 - 25)$.

First, solve the parentheses and exponents.

$12^2 = 144$

$z = 21 + (2 \times 144 - 25)$

Multiply 2 with 144 to obtain 288.

$z = 21 + (288 - 25)$

Even though addition comes first in PEMDAS, you have to subtract first here in order to have something to add.

Subtract 25 from 288 to obtain 263.

Finally, add.

$z = 21 + 263 = 284$.

(21) (C) 60 degrees.

An equilateral triangle has sides of equal lengths. Therefore, all the three interior angles of an equilateral triangle are also equal, which means that each angle of an equilateral triangle will be 60 degrees.

To verify, use the value of the sum of the interior angles of a triangle.

The sum of the interior angles of a triangle is 180 degrees.

Let one unknown interior angle be x.

$60 + x + x = 180$

Subtract 60 from 180 to obtain 120 and add the two xs to obtain 2x.

$2x = 180 - 60$

Divide 120 by 2 to obtain the value of each unknown interior angle, x.

$x = 120/2 = 60$ degrees.

(22) (B) 0.0895 m².

Since the final answer is required in meters, convert the units of the provided measurements.

$1 \text{ cm} = 1/100$ meters

Therefore, 150 cm = 150/100 = 1.5 meters.

The perimeter (circumference) of the circle = $2\pi r$

Substitute the value of the perimeter in the formula and divide it by 2π to obtain the value of the radius, r.

$1.5/2\pi = r = 0.239$ meter

The formula for the area of the circle:

Area of the circle = πr^2

A semicircle is half of the circle. Hence the formula for the area of the semicircle:

Area of the semicircle = $\pi r^2 /2$

Substitute the value of the radius, r, in the formula to find the area of half of the circle.

Area of the semicircle = $\pi (0.239)^2 /2 = 0.0895$ m².

(23) (B) y = -2.

$1/2^{-1}$ can also be written as 2^1.

$1/16^y$ can also be written as 2^{-4y}.

8 can also be written as 2^3.

Hence, the equation can be written as $2^1 \div 2^{-4y} = 2^6 \times 2^3$.

Taking the left-hand side, when the bases of the terms are the same and the terms are divided, their powers subtract from each other.

Taking the right-hand side, when the bases of the terms are the same and the terms are multiplied, their powers add up.

So, the equation can now be written as $2^{1 - 4y} = 2^{6 + 3}$.

If the bases of the terms on both sides of the = sign are the same, their powers are also equal.

So, $1 - 4y = 6 + 3$.

$1 - 4y = 9$

Subtract 1 from 9 to obtain 8.

$-4y = 8$

Divide 8 by -4 to obtain the value of y.

$y = 8/\text{-}4 = \text{-}2$.

(24) (A) 48,000 grams.

To calculate the number of boxes of sweets the couple could not distribute, subtract 5 and 21 from 50.

$50 - 21 - 5 = 24$ boxes

If the mass of one box is 2 kg, the mass of 24 boxes will be $24 \times 2 = 48$ kg.

Since the answer is required in grams, convert the units of the mass obtained.

1 kg = 1,000 grams

Hence, 48 kg = 48 x 1,000 = 48,000 grams. The couple was not able to distribute 48,000 grams of sweets.

(25) (C) A*.

To find Tim's grade, first calculate the percentage he managed to attain.

The formula for calculating the percentage attained:

Percentage attained = (scores obtained/total scorers) x 100

Percentage attained = (75 + 50 + 81 + 93/400) x 100

Percentage attained = (299/400) x 100

Percentage attained = 74.75%

Students who scored 70% or above received an A*. Since Tim attained 74.75% and it is above 70%, he will get an A*.

(26) (A) 561,600 seconds.

If 2 days = 172,800 seconds

Then, 1 day = 172,800/2 = 86,400 seconds

Therefore, 6.5 days = 6.5 x 86,400 = 561,600 seconds.

(27) (B) Scale.

A measuring cylinder is used to measure the volume of liquid, whereas inch tape and meter rulers are used to measure length. However, a scale is used to measure the mass of an object.

(28) (C) Length = 0.08 m; width = 0.2 m.

Since the answer is required in meters, convert the units.

1 cm = 1/100 meters

Therefore, 200 cm = 200/100 = 2 meters.

Let the length of the rectangle be x meters.

Since the width of the rectangle is one-fourth of its length:

Width = 1/4x

The formula for the perimeter of the rectangle:

Perimeter of the rectangle = 2 (length) + 2 (width)

Substitute the value of the perimeter and the expressions for length and width in the formula.

2 = 2 (x) + 2 (x/4)

Simplify 2x/4 into 1x/2.

Take 2 as the LCM on the right-hand side to make the two terms' denominators the same.

2 = (4x + x) /2

Add 4x and x to obtain 5x.

2 = 5x/2

Multiply 2 by 2 and divide it by 5 to obtain the value of x, the length.

4/5 = x = 0.8s meter is the length.

Width = 1/4 (x) = 1/4 (0.8) = 0.2 meters.

(29) (C) 1.

Irrespective of how large or small it is, any number will always be equal to 0 if the power on the number is 0. Therefore, 3456^0 is always equal to 1.

(30) (A) 89/250.

To remove the % sign from 35.6%, divide it by 100 to obtain 35.6/100.

Both 35.6 and 100 are further divisible by 2/5.

35.6 divided by 2/5 is equal to 89, and 100 divided by 2/5 is equal to 250.

Hence, 35.6/100 can also be written as 89/250 as its simplified form.

Test 3: Writing Answers & Explanations

(1) (B) II.

Compare-and-contrast essays discuss the similarities and the differences between two things. Sentence I is a thesis statement, offers a point of view, and does not feature any contrasts. Sentence III is a descriptive statement about a man known as Alfred Wegener; it cannot be used because it features no comparison or contrast. Sentence IV cannot work because it contains no comparison or contrast; it could be used as a precursor to a thesis statement in a persuasive speech or essay.

Only Sentence II can be used as an introduction to a compare-and-contrast essay because it compares the Axis and the Allies and describes the main difference between them.

(2) (A) I.

Argumentative essays discuss the writer's point of view and try to convince the reader that that particular point of view is correct. Sentence II compares the Axis and Allies and describes a difference between them. This sentence would be appropriate in a compare-and-contrast essay but not in an argumentative essay. Sentence III is a descriptive statement about a man known as Alfred Wegener; it cannot be used because it offers no particular point of view. Sentence IV could be used as a precursor to the thesis statement in an argumentative essay. It cannot be used as a thesis statement because it does not offer a particular point of view to the reader.

Thus, Sentence I is the only one that can be used as a thesis statement because it offers an argument for keeping taxes down.

(3) (D) IV.

Persuasive essays discuss the writer's point of view and try to convince the reader that that particular point of view is correct. Sentence I is a thesis statement that presents an argument. Sentence III offers a comparison between two things and can be used only in a compare-and-contrast essay. Sentence III is a descriptive statement about a man known as Alfred Wegener; it cannot be used because it offers no particular point of view and preface about an argument.

Thus, Sentence IV is the only one that can act as the introductory sentence to a persuasive essay because it provides a precursor to the material that could be followed by an argument.

(4) (C) Verb-tense errors.

The paragraph does not contain any capitalization errors, run-on sentences or subject-verb disagreements. It is written in the past tense. Some verbs do not match the tense of the paragraph. In line 2, the present-tense verb *back* conflicts with the past-tense verb *covered*. In line 3, the present-tense verb *sheaths* contrasts with the past-tense verb *sat*.

(5) (A) Hellinistic.

Hellinistic is spelled incorrectly. It should be written as *Hellenistic*.

(6) (D) Revising.

Option A is moot, as Calvin has finished drafting his manuscript. Publishing happens only when the manuscript has been revised and edited. Right now, Calvin has just finished his work, so Option B is also incorrect. In the writing process, editing comes only after extensive revision is done on the manuscript. The revision process comes immediately after drafting. Thus, Option D, revising, is the next step in the writing process.

(7) (B) The renowned jeweler designed the expensive watch and the stunning diamond ring.

Passive voice is when an action is done *to* the subject of the sentence. Active voice is when the subject does an action. In the given sentence, the subject is being acted upon. Option A is incorrect because it only partially changes the passive sentence to active. In Option C, the writer changed only half the sentence to the active voice. The sentence presented in Option D could be correct, but the original sentence is much too changed. Option D is missing some adjectives that were present in the original sentence.

In Option B, the sentence is translated directly into active voice without any new additions.

(8) (D) The Bayley Tower.

The subject of a sentence is the thing or person that is doing or performing an action in the sentence. Subjects are usually nouns (*cat, Henry*), noun phrases (*Stern Review*) or pronouns (*he, she*). Option A is the simple predicate in the sentence, so it cannot be the subject. *Ancient* is an adjective that gives more information about the noun *legend*. *The Bayley Tower* is a proper noun and performs the action in the sentence. Thus, it is the subject.

(9) (C) Books on Roman and Greek culture.

Sienna is writing an essay comparing the Greek and Roman cultures. Using an encyclopedia would not help Sienna make her essay as informative as possible because encyclopedias do not go into the details of anything. Rather, they skim over the surface of every concept they introduce. An article about Greek culture would be unsuitable because Sienna has to find information about Roman culture too. Books based on Roman and Greek culture would be most appropriate, as they would provide her with accurate information and may also provide comparisons. Thus, Sienna should use books on Roman and Greek culture as reference material as she writes her essay.

(10) (A) Invited.

The simple predicate is the verb that tells the reader what the subject is doing or the action a subject is taking. The simple predicate usually comes after the subject. In this case, the predicate is *invited* because it comes after the subject *Shelly*. Thus, Option A is correct.

(11) (D) Verb-tense errors.

There is a verb-tense error in this sentence. The sentence is written in the past tense, as indicated by the presence of the past-tense verbs *stacked* and *was* later in the sentence. The verb *stand* is a present-tense verb, and it does not agree with the tense of the sentence as a whole.

(12) (B) pacific fleet.

Four words are underlined in this sentence. The first option contains no error, nor does it disrupt the sentence. Similarly, no verb-tense errors are present in Option C. Nor are there any comma-usage errors in Option D. However, capitalization errors can be found in Option B. The proper noun *pacific fleet* should have been capitalized to *Pacific Fleet*. A proper noun is a specific name for a person, place, thing or idea. Proper nouns are always capitalized.

(13) (B) was.

In this sentence, the past form *was* of the verb *is* is used instead of the present form. The whole sentence is written in the present tense, as shown by the use of verbs such as *is*. Option B highlights the use of the verb *was*—a past-tense verb. This verb does not agree with the tense and is incorrect.

(14) (B) occurence.

The sentence does not contain any capitalization errors, verb-tense errors, or subject-verb disagreement errors. But, in this complex sentence, the word *occurence* is misspelled. It is missing a second letter *r*. It should be spelled *occurrence*.

(15) (A) confederate states.

Of the options presented in the sentence, Options B, C and D contain no grammatical, punctuation, spelling, or word usage errors. However, Option A has a capitalization error. In this sentence, the proper noun *confederate states* should have been capitalized.

(16) (D) grenery.

The sentence does not contain any capitalization errors, verb-tense errors or subject-verb errors. But the word *grenery* is misspelled. It should be spelled *greenery*.

(17) (B) routed.

The verb *route* means to direct something or someone somewhere, while the verb *root* means that something is embedded deeply. These words are homophones—words that sound similar. In this case, the word *root* should have been used as a verb in place of the word *route*.

(18) (D) Orographic or relief rainfall happens when air is forced to rise over a mountain or any barrier, and is forced to cool down, condense, and form rain.

All punctuation in Options A, B and C is correctly used. There are no commas in Options A and D. In Option B, both the commas are correctly used. The comma that appears after the word *barrier* in Option D is incorrectly used, as it separates the subject of the sentence from the verb.

(19) (C) A verb.

The part of speech that is underlined in this sentence is a verb. It cannot be a quantifier because it does not specify the amount of something; it is not an adverb because it does not modify another verb or adjective. Nor is it an adjective because it does not give extra information.

(20) (B) There are two types of deserts in the world: hot and cold.

Of the four options presented, Option A is a run-on sentence with a comma splice between the sentences. Option D is incorrect because a semicolon is used between a phrase and a sentence fragment. In Option C, a semicolon is used between an independent clause and a phrase. Option B is the correct option as it joins both the sentence parts without any grammatical mistakes.

(21) (D) Comma.

A semicolon is used to connect two independent clauses that are related. Sentence 8 is independent, while sentence 9 is dependent, or a sentence fragment. Hence, they cannot be connected by a semicolon. The conjunction *and* is usually used to connect two independent clauses. Since sentence 9 is not an independent sentence, the conjunction *and* cannot be used. The conjunction *that* is used to connect a dependent clause to a sentence when the dependent clause is essential to the meaning of the sentence as a whole. Unfortunately, *that* cannot be used between these two sentences due to the present progressive form of the verb *ranging* in sentence 9. Hence, the comma the punctuation mark Dylan can use to connect his sentence.

(22) (B) It is extremely dry, averaging around 6.5 inches of precipitation every year.

The first option cannot be used because it has information that is relevant to the Sahara Desert, not the Antarctic. Option C cannot be used because it does not offer information that is relevant to the claims made in the sentence. Option D is a statement that contains no supporting details that could be added to the paragraph. Thus, only Option B can be used as a good supporting detail.

(23) (C) Yes, because the sentence repeats information that is already mentioned elsewhere in the essay.

At this point, this sentence does not add anything to the essay; rather, it repeats the information already presented in the previous paragraph. Thus, it should be removed from the paragraph.

(24) (B) The first time she saw a baby macaw, she was mesmerized: it had a small, hard beak; colorful red green and blue dappled feathers; and little tiny feet.

Of all the options presented in this question, Options A, C and D are grammatically correct and have no comma errors. Option B has a comma missing in the second series, "colorful red green and blue dappled feathers." The comma is missing between *red* and *green*.

(25) (D) Verb-tense errors.

In this sentence, the present form of the verb *glide* is used instead of the past form *glided*. This verb does not agree with the tense and is incorrect. The whole sentence is written in the past tense, as shown by the use of verbs such as *walked* and *was*. The verb *glided* should be used in place of *glides*.

(26) (D) Pinacle.

Pinacle is misspelled. It should be written as *pinnacle*.

(27) (A) Proofreading.

The question tells us that Kevin has finished the final draft of his thesis. This means that he has drafted his work and revised it a few times already. At this moment, Kevin is using Track Changes in Word to correct any punctuation errors. Checking the work for typos, tense errors and all other superficial errors is the last step in the writing process. It is called proofreading. It is different from editing because editing is a more in-depth process that can result in big changes to improve the work. Proofreading focuses on checking the text for grammatical accuracy and any typing errors.

(28) (B) A biography of Niccolò Machiavelli.

Of all the options presented, Option A would not provide Gilliam with the information she wants because encyclopedias do not provide in-depth information about any topic. Articles do not contain enough information that Gilliam could use in her paper. Since Gilliam is writing a paper, she needs primary reference material. An atlas would be useless for Gilliam's purposes because atlases offer maps and geographical information but will not provide any information about the famous philosopher. A biography about Niccolò Machiavelli would be good because it would provide enough information about his life, it would be accurate, and it could discuss the reasons Niccolò's literary work became very famous.

(29) (D) Incorrect word usage.

The verb *reined* means you kept something under control or curbed some impulse, while the verb *reigned* means ruled as monarch. These words are homophones—words that sound similar. In this case, *reigned* should have been used as a verb in place of *reined*.

(30) (B) Solisits.

Solisits is spelled incorrectly. It should be written as *solicits*.

Essay Question: Sample Response

Every year, countless high school and college students are caught and expelled based on cheating. Many suffer severe consequences due to one misdemeanor.

Should cheaters, if caught, be given another chance?

All students are taught at school that they should not copy other students' work or peek at another student's exam. If they still commit these acts, then they will surely fail the assessment, as the teacher will suspend them for cheating. In some outrageous cheating cases, students are expelled from their school for cheating. However, in some cases, the judgments are too harsh and can lead to terrible consequences for the cheater. Thus, it is better to give one more chance to a student who has cheated on a test or an assignment before considering expulsion.

First of all, students who cheat on assignments or tests should not be expelled from school but should be severely penalized. It is a human quality to make mistakes, but anyone who keeps making the same mistake should earn the consequences of their actions. Students should be taught the consequences of their actions by having severe penalties enforced on them. If these students are let go without any reprimand, they will not learn the lesson that cheating is disrespectful to themselves, their friends and their teachers. They will cheat again if they feel that there will be no repercussions for their actions. They may learn that cheating is an easier way to skate through the world and may start cheating in their professional lives, alienating themselves from their colleagues.

Secondly, expulsion can destroy a student's life. Contrary to popular opinion, most students do not cheat because they are lazy. Most of the time, students lack confidence, are extremely desperate or are so distressed that they resort to cheating because they think they will not pass on their own accord.

Immediate expulsion after getting caught cheating can make the student's chances of getting into another school very difficult. Later on, without a degree, getting a well-paying job will be almost impossible. If a person cannot complete a high school diploma, he or she will not be qualified to go to college, and nowadays, most jobs are given to holders of bachelor's degrees and above. Besides, expelling students without giving them a chance to correct their mistakes makes it more likely the students will cheat again because they find it an easier alternative to studying.

On the other hand, at times, giving a cheater a second chance is risky, especially in higher grades. If a student made one mistake, then he or she should be given a chance. But a track record of cheating with no repercussions at higher grades enables these students to get into college rather than someone who worked hard.

Similarly, giving cheaters a second chance raises the question of trust. How can compulsive cheaters be trusted if they make the same mistake again and again? How can a doctor or engineer or a lawyer who cheats be trusted? How will these people help other people if they do not follow the basic ethics of their profession? These are all questions to ask when allowing a cheater a second chance.

In conclusion, expelling students for being caught cheating once will not help them learn; rather, it will create more problems for the students later in life because they might not be able to get into college or get a well-paying job after their expulsion. However, giving a second chance to a cheater can be risky if the student is in a higher grade. All in all, instead of expulsion, students should be taught how to complete their assignments, and if they are unable to do so, they should be offered help through student unions or their class teachers.

CPSIA information can be obtained
at www.ICGtesting.com
Printed in the USA
BVHW061201280722
643248BV00011B/420